CLOSURE:
THE LIE WE TELL
OURSELVES

Kimberly Isherwood

CLOSURE:
THE LIE WE TELL OURSELVES

A MEMOIR ABOUT INTUITION, HEALING, AND EMBRACING LIFE'S UNCERTAINTIES.

KIMBERLY ISHERWOOD

NEW DEGREE PRESS
COPYRIGHT © 2023 KIMBERLY ISHERWOOD
All rights reserved.

CLOSURE: THE LIE WE TELL OURSELVES
A memoir about intuition, healing, and embracing life's uncertainties.

ISBN   979-8-88926-945-8   *Paperback*
            979-8-88926-988-5   *Ebook*

This book is dedicated to all the beautiful souls who have shared their stories with me. May this book serve as a reminder that we are all connected in ways we may not fully comprehend. May it inspire us to live fully, love deeply and appreciate every day we have together.

CONTENTS

	AUTHOR'S NOTE	11
	INTRODUCTION	13

PART I	**THE JOURNEY**	**19**
CHAPTER 1	HOW IT ALL BEGAN	21
CHAPTER 2	THE LONG ROAD TO KNOWING	29
CHAPTER 3	LIFELINES	37
CHAPTER 4	THE WEIGHT OF CARING	45
CHAPTER 5	WATER CHANGED ME	53
CHAPTER 6	YOU'RE A WHAT? THE WORK OF AN INTUITIVE MEDIUM	69

PART II	**THEIR STORIES**	**79**
CHAPTER 7	DREW AND KATHERINE	81
CHAPTER 8	GORDON	89
CHAPTER 9	MACKENZIE	97
CHAPTER 10	ABBIE	107
CHAPTER 11	CARMEN	115
CHAPTER 12	PAUL	127
CHAPTER 13	ALEX AND KATE	137

PART III	**TOOLS, TECHNIQUES, AND FRIENDLY ADVICE FOR DEALING WITH GRIEF**	**147**
CHAPTER 14	TOOLS, TECHNIQUES, AND FRIENDLY ADVICE FOR DEALING WITH GRIEF	149
	CONCLUSION	155
	ACKNOWLEDGMENTS	159
	APPENDIX	163

*"Unable are the Loved to die/
For Love is Immortality..."*

—EMILY DICKINSON

AUTHOR'S NOTE

This book is a compilation of stories and conversations from my experiences as an intuitive medium, wife, mother, and friend. I have welcomed the characters in these stories into my life, my home, and my heart. Clients, family, and friends come to me because they need help. They come for answers, clarity, or solace. Most of them say they are looking for closure, and I recoil from that word every single time. Grief, heartbreak, loss, and healing all come in unique ways, and they progress differently over time.

The stories in this book contain topics which may be triggering for you: death, depression, suicide, natural disaster, pregnancy and infant loss, divorce, and emotional trauma. They are stories that are difficult for those who lived through these experiences, and they may be difficult to read, but they are stories that need to be heard.

I hope that you see yourself or someone you know in these pages, and they help you to find a new way of looking at grief. I hope that it will soften your heart if you love someone whose grief makes you feel uncomfortable. I hope that this book gives you permission to feel deeply and grieve on your own terms for as little or as long as you want. More than anything, I hope you will let go of the mythical idea that closure is the answer.

Only when we feel safe can we discuss the hardest moments of our lives. Only when we feel that our trust will be honored can we fully express our truth. This work depicts actual events as truthfully as recollection permits. Many of my clients have graciously offered to share their sessions in the writing of this book or have sat for interviews, and for that I am humbled and forever grateful. The stories in this book are based on real people and events, but all names, locations, and identifying details have been changed, and some stories have been combined to protect the privacy of the individuals involved. The only exceptions are my own stories, which I share generously and honestly.

INTRODUCTION

Psychics. Is there any real value in what they tell us?

Since medieval times, kings and queens have consulted soothsayers and spiritual guides. Queen Elizabeth I employed Dr. John Dee, a noted British mathematician and astronomer who devoted much of his life to alchemy, divination, and hermetic philosophy. He frequently used crystal balls in his divination and astrology in his work (Bevan 2023). Early Nordic and Germanic tribes of northern Europe used runes as early as 300 AD (World History Encyclopedia 2018), and tarot cards have been used for readings since the late 1800s. Over time, spiritualism and esoteric practices have shifted from seances in dark parlors to mainstream celebrations with beautiful sound healing ceremonies and meditation circles in the light of day.

Metaphysical services are more accepted now than ever. It is estimated that the psychic services market in the U.S. will generate $2.3 billion in revenue in 2023 (IBISWorld 2021). Metaphysical shops are now commonplace. Palmistry, aura readings, crystals, and tarot cards are no longer feared as dangerous or satanic. There are many opportunities to seek help and guidance in entirely new ways, but not everyone in the industry is in it for the greater good of all involved. Some are opportunists, and that is frustrating for those of us who do this work with integrity.

I am an intuitive medium, and I know there is value in what I do, but I also know there are complications that come with that. For more than a decade, I have had the privilege of holding sacred space and providing intuitive readings for hundreds of individuals. Almost daily, a new client will call to schedule a session and inevitably, they say, "I need closure."

Humans hate uncertainty. We want reassurance that a late loved one is okay or that their death was quick. We want to know how to move on from our pain. The idea of closure suggests an end to pain and a life after trauma. The word is used daily in therapy sessions and in courtrooms. It is also a major marketing tool leveraged by the funeral industry. But my experience has shown me closure—at least the way we think of it—isn't possible. It's a mythical, abstract idea that does not exist. It is a short-term salve to a burn that is forever in our physical, emotional, and energetic selves.

For years, I wanted to write this book, but something always held me back. In addition to my work as a medium, I am also a registered nurse who has worked in Intensive Care and Cardiology for many years. I have witnessed patients pulled back from the brink of death and held the hand of many as they took their last breath. Throughout my career, my rules included do no harm, live your life in service, and always follow the rules of science. Writing a book about closure, which is a topic the psychology community holds sacred, is a risky business, and one that I do not take lightly.

In 2019, after years of witnessing the grief of others, my husband and I experienced a disaster firsthand. We were in the path of the one-hundred-year flood that destroyed thousands of homes along the Platte and Missouri rivers. The devastation of that flood changed me forever. I thought I knew about the unbearable weight of PTSD and trauma. I thought I knew what panic attacks and grief felt like before, but now I know them intimately as I learned to cope with the roller-coaster of emotions that come unexpectedly at the worst times. During the flood, no one in my family died; we rebuilt and moved on. But the trauma created by the fear and devastation of the wild, muddy water is still deep in my bones.

The flood shifted my perspective. I see PTSD, grief, and emotional pain through a different lens. Our society expects that when something terrible happens, we *should* grieve…just not too much lest we become clinically depressed. And we should be "over it" after a reasonable, yet short, amount of time. And within a certain respectable number of weeks, we should be past the sadness. And after a handful of months, we should have moved through the alleged "stages" of grieving and be back in the swing of things.

I disagree. Grief is infinite. Grief is malleable and tricky, a permanent part of us, and it changes constantly. Closure would be nice if it were real. Closure would be a way out of this story, but closure is the lie we tell ourselves.

In June of 2022, three weeks into writing this book, a dear friend died by suicide. Her death has been absolutely devastating. Each week, I hoped to write about her from a different perspective, but my emotions make it extremely difficult. I am grieving for her as I write, still wrestling with the fact that she no longer exists on this earth plane. I miss her and, like anyone who loves someone who has died by suicide, I feel the pain of a love with nowhere to go. Even though she left a letter and was very clear about her reasons, I am sure there are others grieving for her who want answers and feel that, with those answers, they can find closure. I hope to honor her with this book. She will float amongst many of these pages, and I will tell our story as I experienced it. Our journey together continues, but hopefully in a way that will help others. I know she would have wanted that.

This book is for anyone who has experienced grief. It is for anyone who has experienced the death of a close family member or friend, whether it was by suicide, illness, or injury. It is for partnered humans, whether married or in a love relationship, and for people who have experienced a divorce or breakup and continue to hold on to unanswered questions. It is for therapists and grief counselors who are still using closure as a method of processing grief. It is for anyone who has been physically or emotionally traumatized and is still healing.

This book is a permission slip to see the emotions related to grief differently. It is a collection of stories from my life as an intuitive medium and stories from sessions and interviews I have had the honor of sharing. These stories offer a way to see that as we become familiar with our reactions and responses to uncomfortable moments, we can take grief along on our journey. It can join us as part of our team, but we don't have to let it run the show.

Part 1 is my personal journey through embracing my intuitive abilities and facing the many challenges real life put in my path.

Part 2 is a collection of stories and interviews from clients, friends, and acquaintances with whom I have worked with over the years. Their stories illustrate how we've worked through their grief and other difficult situations.

Part 3 includes tools and advice that can help move us through different chapters of our grief and emotions. These tools are common sense, easily accessible things that anyone can try. You don't have to be an intuitive medium or a yogi for these tools to help. In fact, my hope is that you develop trust in yourself, and you honor your own emotions and feelings in a way that feels healthy and strong for you.

Your grief is uniquely your own and you do not need to seek closure. Closure is bullshit.

PART I

THE JOURNEY

Part 1 is a deeply personal account of my journey towards accepting and embracing my intuitive gifts. For many years, I struggled to understand and trust the subtle nudges and insights that I received from beyond the physical realm. In this section, I share my experiences of overcoming self-doubt and fear to tap into my intuitive abilities and how this journey transformed my life.

These chapters contain topics which may be triggering, including the death of a child, suicide, depression, and post-traumatic stress disorder.

CHAPTER 1

HOW IT ALL BEGAN

Down a cobblestone street and through a narrow alley, hides a place that one can go for answers. The word "psychic" is illuminated in neon orange in the otherwise-dimly lit window of a shop. Upon entering, one is greeted with the smell of sage and frankincense. A tiny old woman in a purple, velvet shawl sits behind a small round table. The woman's bony hands shuffle a deck of tarot cards as stacks of silver bracelets clink on her wrists. The old crone looks up with cloudy eyes and greets visitors with a gravelly voice.

"Come in, my darling. I am Madame Sophia, and I've been waiting for you."

Tales of fortune tellers and psychics popularize characters who warn of dangers that lurk ahead and traverse unknown realms. They are mysterious and intriguing, and they could not be more different from me.

I am a wife, mother, grandmother, writer, nurse, and yoga teacher. I live my life like most people in the Midwest, but I have a special talent. I am an intuitive medium. I see, feel, hear, and know things, and then I channel them. In truth, I struggle with the word psychic. It just doesn't sit right on my brain or heart when describing myself, so I use the word intuitive instead. I'm not a wise old crone who can dance between magical realms. Most days, I spend more time than I would like looking for my eternally lost reading glasses and cell phone. My intuitive abilities are absolutely no help for the simple problems that plague mankind.

I have not always known I was intuitive. It has taken years of work, meditation, therapy, and mentorship to become comfortable with it.

I was raised in a small town in western Nebraska by parents with very opposite views of organized religion. My mother loved the community that church provided. My father felt organized religion was the source of far too many conflicts in the world and wanted nothing to do with it. Growing up, I attended a local church with my mother. I did and still do appreciate aspects of my church experience, but hurtful experiences there left a deep mark on my soul and impacted my early understanding of my own intuition.

"Sin is the devil's work. Do not take the Lord's name in vain or the wrath of God will be upon thee," Reverend Kelly would bellow from his pulpit. "Be devout in your faith and live without sin or you shall surely face the fire and damnation of eternal hell." Reverend Kelly's sermons had a constant thread: *The devil is always lurking around. Don't do anything bad because if you do, you are absolutely, unequivocally going to hell.* Hell was always a consequence for even the slightest misstep. All those words put the fear of God in me.

Though exciting things rarely happened in our small, Midwestern town, the nightly news would argue otherwise. The sixties and seventies were the time of the Vietnam war, the energy crisis, and the killer bees. More reasons for fearful nightly prayers from an anxious prepubescent girl.

Going to the movies was a primary source of entertainment in our town, and the drive-in theater was packed bumper to bumper on summer nights. Horror movies were all the rage. My mother would shriek and cover her eyes during scary moments and my dad would laugh as my brothers and I hid behind the front seat waiting to get the signal from my mom that it was okay to look. Parental ratings weren't really a consideration in those days.

In 1971, *The Exorcist* was published, which was a game changer. My best friend Kathy's mom read it, and one night, Kathy and I snuck into her parent's bedroom and took her mother's copy from the nightstand. We knew we weren't supposed to read it, but our curiosity overcame us. We were sure we could handle it.

After reading a book which no eleven-year-old should ever read, I was scared to death of the devil possessing me. Perhaps it was the combination of all those Satan sermons in church and the vivid depiction of Reagan and her contorted body and pea-green vomit that tortured me the most. *The Exorcist* was a powder keg and my vivid imagination the match. It set off what would now most definitely be diagnosed as anxiety. I'm not sure if William Peter Blatty had set out to scare the living hell out of millions with his work, but *The Exorcist* certainly had that effect. In client sessions today, many people reference their fears of being possessed by the devil coming directly from that book or its film adaption.

It was around that time I started feeling like someone was in my room. It felt like a presence was trying to get close to me. I was incredibly scared. I had my own bedroom on the second floor of our little bungalow house, and at night after turning off my light, I would feel a tall brown column of energy much like a person standing near my bed.

"Now I lay me down to sleep, I pray the Lord my soul to keep. And if I die before I wake, I pray the Lord my soul to take," I would whisper under my covers over and over again. Religion, my sensitivity, and now horror stories were creating a toxic stew in my little body. I prayed this spirit, or whatever it was, would go away. When it got too scary, I would jump out of bed and run as fast as I could down the stairs and into my parent's bedroom.

"There's someone in my room. I'm scared," I would tell my parents, trying hard not to cry. Crying was a very bad thing in my home and rarely tolerated by my parents.

"There's no one in your room," my mom would answer. "Go back to bed. You are dreaming." She always blamed everything on bad dreams.

"No, no, I can't. I'm too scared. This thing is going to get me," I pleaded, sure that it was the devil, and he was about to take my soul.

"Get in with us or sleep on the couch," my dad said as he flipped open the covers, and I would crawl in. I rarely took the couch option, but there was no way I was going back to my room with that spirit lurking around, ready to take my soul.

After suffering through the nightly routine of praying, seeing a spirit, being scared to death, and rushing into my parents' bedroom, no one in the house was sleeping well. My mother called the new pastor of our church and asked him to come to our house and help us through this crisis. Pastor Johnson came after school one afternoon and sat down with me in our living room. First we prayed, and then we talked about what had been happening. In very short order, he determined that a Ouija board I had been given as a Christmas gift was the problem.

"You have allowed dark and demonic energies to enter the house through this board. It's a dangerous tool and one you have no business using," he said as he looked in my eyes and held both of my hands in his. He was very kind during his visit, and I trusted every word he said. I wanted help. I wanted him to be right. I wanted all the scary stuff to go away. How was I to know that I had been messing with something dangerous? I was just a kid. I had thought the Ouija board was just a fun thing we did with friends during slumber parties.

"You need to come to church regularly, pray with all your heart, and join the youth choir. They need voices like yours," he said. I believed him. When he walked out of our house with my Ouija board under his arm, I had no doubt that he had all the answers. I did all the things he had told me to do. I went to church every Sunday and I got baptized. The full-body-under-the-water baptism, not just a few drops of water on my head. I went all in. I sang in the choir, I read the Bible, and I prayed with all my heart, but it didn't stop. I never stopped sensing the tall brown presence in my room, so I kept it to myself. I was constantly afraid, but I didn't tell anyone. I believed I was the problem.

I don't remember specifically when the spirit stopped showing up, or when I stopped feeling scared. Perhaps it was just a normal process of maturing or becoming distracted with other things like chasing boys. Our family moved to a different house when I was in high school, and I worked at the local hospital as a nurse's aide and later went on to college and received my nursing degree. It was a challenging career with many highs and lows. I felt loss and death deeply when it happened. I learned to compartmentalize those deep, painful feelings and carry on with the work that needed to be done. At age twenty-three, I moved to Colorado and worked in the local hospital's intensive care unit.

In my off hours, I found a metaphysical community that was alive and welcoming. I studied meditation and attended weekend sit-ins where groups meditated together at the foot of beautiful mountains. I began to realize that my intuitive abilities were not something to be feared. I began to explore my inner sense of knowing. I reveled in conversations with like-minded humans who talked about astral projection and past lives the way friends shared recipes in my hometown. It was like learning to breathe in an entirely new way. I embraced my intuition and the parts of myself that I had been shamed for as a child. I was still very much on a path of seeking answers and clarity, but it all felt right to me.

Meanwhile, I met a guy from my hometown, we fell in love, and a year later we were married. At twenty-five, I moved back to Nebraska and quickly discovered the metaphysical world I had found so welcoming in Colorado didn't exist there. It hadn't been an environment that nurtured my metaphysical self in the past, but now the contrast was blatant. There were no meditation groups, drum circles, or crystal shops, but there were lots of churches.

An entire part of me shut down.

CHAPTER 2

THE LONG ROAD TO KNOWING

"You are crazy. I don't hear anything. The house is settling," my husband responded condescendingly when I asked him if he had heard the banging. We had been standing alone in the kitchen of our one-hundred-year-old farmhouse and I had heard footsteps above us.

Most of our conversations about my gut feelings were met with condescension.

"You're not psychic, you're psycho."

I hated those words. I heard them from him often. We had been renovating the old house for months and the more walls we opened up, the more I heard noises, footsteps on wooden floors, and doors opening and slamming. The house was active, and I could feel it. I knew what I was experiencing was not in my imagination. My husband disagreed.

Our daughter was born four months after we moved into the dilapidated house. We continued to work tirelessly to make it functional again. It was backbreaking work, and during those years, the house became symbolic of our life together. It was livable, but never quite right. Our son was born three years later, but our marriage was rocky, and life was hard inside those walls.

After nine years together, our marriage ended in a very difficult divorce. Difficult is an understatement: it was a *horrendous* divorce. The children and I left the old house and began the painful process of rebuilding our lives and I became a thirty-four-year-old single mom. I dove into my career in the medical field and used my morning commute to listen to every book on Oprah's book club list. The weekends my children were with their father, I headed straight to the self-help aisle of Barnes and Noble. I devoured everything I could find to help shore up all the broken parts of myself. I was looking for answers and a way to end my emotional pain. Books were my solace.

Life got better when I fell in love with a kind man who made me laugh every day. He loved me for me, he loved my kids, and in 2000, we were married. He had dreamed of being a doctor and, in 2002, he was accepted to the University of Nebraska, and we were ecstatic. During his time in med school and residency, I left my job in medical practice management and took a position in medical device sales, which was a whole new world. I had to learn electrophysiology, business plans, and spreadsheets. Years passed, and raising children and meeting the challenges of a tough job were taking a toll. I needed balance, stress management, and a way to deal with the bad back I had acquired from my time as a nurse. I went back to yoga and meditation.

The more mature and battle-worn forty-six-year-old version of myself welcomed the discipline of yoga like the embrace of an old friend. It was exactly what my body, mind and spirit had been longing for. Yoga was in stark contrast to the corporate demands that I faced during the day, and I loved all that it offered.

In 2007, my yoga teacher became my business partner and together, we purchased a yoga studio in downtown Omaha. It was in a beautiful old building with squeaky stairs and stained-glass windows. It was a dream come true. I taught yoga and lead meditation classes and I wanted to go even deeper into the discipline. It was a calling. I looked for teachers, mentors, spirituality classes, and every opportunity that I could find to help guide me in my search for my energetic growth and expansion. I received Reiki sessions, went to meditation groups and drum circles. I tried it all. I was open to everything.

Our yoga studio was located on the second floor of a historic building and while there, I began to sense the spirit of a young man lurking about in the hallway between our classrooms. I was startled, then curious. His energy felt gregarious. Over time, he became less scary and more like a welcome visitor. My intuitive self was reawakening.

Through it all, my meditation practice was the foundation for everything. For four years, I would sit down each morning, light a candle, settle into the moment, and meditate.

I would start each meditation by allowing my mind to become quiet, and without fail, the first thing I would hear was "First, heal thyself."

As an obedient student and seeker, I tried to do just that. I continued the work of healing myself and allowing every layer of my psychic and emotional self to become more familiar. Much like learning a yoga pose, the body at first feels wobbly and the mind disconnected, but with practice, beautiful moments can be achieved. Meditation and focused energy work strengthened my confidence and my sense of knowing, or *clairsentience*, became more accurate. My intuition became more focused, and I trusted the messages and symbols that appeared to me in meditation and in conversations with others. People who had died, places, names, and information came to me easily as I allowed myself to open up, and my walls came down.

One day, I sat down to meditate. I followed my usual routine. I let myself become still and those old familiar words didn't come. I didn't hear, "First, heal thyself."

"Wait, did I miss something?"

I got still again, but the message didn't come. Panic ran through me. Had I lost my connection with energy or source? What was I to do now? How was I to proceed? I had been working on myself and meditating for years and I knew my intuitive abilities were becoming really accurate. I had nurtured my ability to raise my vibration and I wanted to help or serve in some way, but I was scared to share the messages I was receiving intuitively. Who did I think I was, Sandra

Brown? What if I was wrong? Why would anyone ever listen to me?

Those three words never came back as I continued to meditate daily, but I needed clarity on dealing with my self-doubt and major feelings of imposter syndrome, so I reached out to an intuitive who I trusted. Jody was down to earth, sweet, and incredibly intuitive. I called her and we planned to meet at the Panera in Council Bluffs for coffee and a chat.

"I know I have intuitive abilities," I said, "but I'm not sure if I'm at the place where I should be doing readings or sharing them with other people."

She was still for a moment. "Well, if you want to do this, let's do it right now. You're going to do a reading on me right here, right now. If you're ready, it'll be fine. If you're not, then you know you have some work to do," she said, as calmly as if she were negotiating with a plumber on a price to fix the pipes.

I immediately panicked. How could I do an intuitive reading in Panera? How could I do an intuitive reading when there were other people nearby ordering streusel and coffee? What kind of parallel universe had I just gone into? Why did I ask her to meet me? I could name a hundred reasons why this was a terrible idea, but I had asked for clarity and the universe had laid it right out in front of me with a pastry on the side.

"Umm. Okay," I stammered. My heart was racing, and I felt sweaty and hot. I was completely unprepared.

"Okay, let's do it," Jody said as she pulled out a sheet of paper and green pencil from her bag. "I'll jot things down while you're talking, and we will see what comes through." I felt like I was standing in the middle of a stage with a spotlight shining in my face, but I took a breath, focused in on Jody and the light around her, and began to speak, "I see an older woman in a tweed coat. She's tiny and she's holding this huge sheet pan full of cake or bars of some kind. Pumpkin bars. She's showing me pumpkin bars."

Jody scribbled down notes and sketched the images I was describing as they were moving through my mind for the next thirty minutes. It felt exhilarating and horrifying at the same time. She was as stoic as a judge and gave me no clues that I was on the right track or completely full of shit. I wanted her to nod or wrinkle her nose, or give me anything, but she didn't. She made me own every moment of our session.

When I felt that the reading was finished, I looked at her drawings and the words she had written as I spoke and felt exhilaration, as though I had just jumped out of an airplane. "So, how did I do?"

Jody smiled and answered. "You have a gift, and you should let it guide you. Just trust me when I say you are psychic. That was the most accurate reading I have ever had." She slid the paper across the table and casually picked up the chocolate chip muffin that had sat untouched for the past half hour and took a bite. "You described my grandmother perfectly. She was known for taking huge pans of cakes to church. Your information was spot on. You don't need to doubt yourself."

I was struggling to process everything that had just happened. Someone I trusted was confirming that I was intuitive, and she had no reason to lie. My first real intuitive reading was a success, and it had happened in the last place I would ever have expected it to unfold. That summer morning at a Panera was a turning point in my life. Validation, confirmation, and honesty were Jody's gifts to me. There was no going back.

I have had no single defining moment in which I realized I was intuitive. Instead, it has been confirmed to me through a million little magical moments along the way. My sense of clarity and confidence have grown with practice. I liken it to learning to play a musical instrument. It starts simple: a few notes, then chords, and eventually music flows effortlessly. I have nurtured my abilities and over time, they have become second nature. I have learned to trust what I feel and know. I listen to my inner voice, and I share what I hear with others when and where I decide it's okay.

I am still growing and evolving and living a wonderful life, but after ten years and hundreds of readings, I am comfortable knowing I am not psycho. I am psychic.

CHAPTER 3

LIFELINES

TW: Suicide, Trauma, Depression

I sense a person's lifeline much like a graph from a seismogram. It appears in my mind with squiggles and scratches. When something important happens, it leaves an obvious mark or a deep cleave much like a cataclysmic earthquake would appear on a seismograph.

If I look back on my own lifeline, there is one event that shook my world and left an indelible mark on my story. Just before my eleventh birthday, my aunt Lily gave birth to a beautiful baby boy, Michael.

Lily was only twelve years older than me, and I adored her. I grew up loving her as more of an older sister than an aunt. Many of my fondest memories are of spending weekends at my grandparents' house, when Lily and I would wake up on Saturday mornings to watch *American Bandstand*. We sang and danced together and every moment we shared felt like an adventure.

When Lily was nineteen, she fell in love with a soft-spoken man named David. He was handsome with thick, always-wild, strawberry-blond hair. He was a veteran of the Vietnam war, and he often wore his green fatigue jacket with his last-name patch on his left breast pocket. After they were married, I didn't understand why I couldn't spend the night at their house. It wasn't until years later that I fully grasped the reality of PTSD: David had night terrors and became violent in his sleep.

On the day Aunt Lily and Michael were to come home from the hospital, David wrote a note, started the car inside of the garage, and died by suicide. Nothing was ever the same again. I watched my beautiful aunt become someone different. The weight of her grief molded her into an entirely different version of the person she had been before David died. The trauma and depression David had tried so desperately to protect his family from became Lily's.

I will never forget his funeral. The funeral home was dimly lit and at each end of his coffin stood two standing lamps. His face and hands looked waxy and unnatural. His wild, wavy hair had been combed too neatly. We later stood amongst rows of white headstones in the military cemetery, and I jumped with each round fired of the ten-gun salute. The folded flag was handed to someone other than his wife.

My aunt, the Lily I knew, wasn't at the funeral that day, and years later the family spoke of her unending grief in judgmental whispers. My grandmother always said, "She just never got over it." How does one get over something that horrendous? The conversations about Lily's mental health shifted over the years and the jargon changed, but the judgement did not.

When I asked her about David's death, my mother explained that because "Lily didn't go to the funeral, she didn't get closure."

This has always sat wrong with me, and it fueled my curiosity about the rules of grief and the fallacy of closure. How did the societal expectation of grief change, and where did the concept of closure come from? When did it enter the ethos?

In tracking the lifeline of closure as a concept, it first appears in the early 1900s as one of the six core principals of Gestalt Psychology. According to Gestalt psychologists, the experience of closure is the result of the mind's tendency to complete incomplete figures, patterns, or objects from the whole. This filling-in process is guided by a set of rules, including the principles of symmetry, continuity, and proximity (Cherry 2021). When the human eye sees an incomplete image or object, the mind will fill in the spaces between and see the complete object. For example, if an image of an incomplete circle appears, humans will infer that it is a circle. Rarely would a person describe the image as a curving line that has two distinct ends that do not connect. This principle is part of the inherent sorting mechanisms in our brains. Humans like familiar patterns, completions, and resolutions. It allows the thousands of stimuli our brain receives each moment to be processed quickly and easily.

In 1969, Swiss psychologist Elizabeth Kubler-Ross published *On Death and Dying*. Her book revolutionized the care of terminally ill patients and hospice care. It was embraced internationally by the medical and psychiatric communities. Kubler-Ross's five stages of death and dying laid out a framework for the emotional responses that could be expected as a person is diagnosed with a terminal illness (Kubler-Ross 1969). The stages include denial, anger, bargaining, depression, and acceptance. The last and final stage, acceptance, refers to coming to terms with one's mortality with objectivity and a sense of resignation. Kubler-Ross's work became precedent primarily because there was at the time very little research and no other framework to describe the grief of terminal illness. The five stages became the one and only road map for death and dying.

So how did closure become the anthem of grief? How did it become the end goal for all pain? I found hundreds of resources about closure and grief, but no one person is formally credited for coining the word. The use of the term seems to have emerged in the pop-psychology era of the nineties. As grief work and grief counseling became more mainstream and self-help became popularized, the bereaved sought closure en masse.

Somehow, Kubler-Ross's stage of acceptance and the pop-psychology destination of closure became indistinguishable from one another. Closure became an act or a ritual that would lead to a tangible end of grief. The psychology and medical communities now use it to comfort those left after a death. Reporters, politicians, lawyers, and judges use it to justify harsh sentences and the death penalty. Funeral directors use it to sell very expensive metal boxes and ceremonies. Police use it when the body of a missing person must be found. Closure has become a manipulative rhetoric.

Grief became fodder for daytime talk shows. Oprah, Montel, Dr. Phil, Jenny Jones, and many other hosts brought out families who were grieving after tragedies and displayed their pain for all to see. The more horrific and salacious the story, the more likely it was to be aired on TV. In 1995, the O.J. Simpson trial was broadcast, and court TV became ratings gold. The emergence of crime and court dramas exploded on primetime television. The tidy Perry Masons of TV law drama became the gritty and hard-hitting *Law and Order*. The lingo of crime, victimization, trauma, and resolution has been wrapped up into one-hour episodes and they normalize the use of the word "closure."

The heft that closure carries is astounding. Little has been documented on the long-term effects of individuals who do not achieve closure. Jody Lynee Madeira's research and 2012 publication of the book *Killing McVeigh* is one of the most comprehensive analyses of closure to date and one of the most conclusive pieces of evidence that the search for closure is a wild goose chase.

In 1995, Timothy McVeigh detonated a two-ton truck bomb in front of the Alfred P. Murrah Federal Building and murdered 168 people, including nineteen children, and injured hundreds of others. It remains the worst act of domestic terrorism in US history. In *Killing McVeigh*, Madeira documents the results of her study of families and survivors of the bombing. She documents the survivors fifteen years after the horrific event. In this poignant compilation of human experiences and data, Madeira shows how the use of the word "closure" was manipulative and oversimplified by both the victims and those interacting with them in some capacity.

Closure was a desired end that all parties involved hoped to experience, but even after viewing McVeigh's execution, few felt a sense of finality that they had hoped for. Closure was not a real state of being; it was an elusive hoax.

> When the term stands before us, naked and stripped of its monstrosity, what do we see? First, closure is most affirmatively not what contemporary culture says it is—absolute finality, in the sense of such colloquial phrases as "over and done with," "dealt with," "put behind one's self," "let bygones be bygones," "forgive and forget." Closure is not a state of being, a quality or even a realization. If closure exists at all, it must be as a process, a recursive series of adjustments that a self makes in response to external, often institutional, developments. It involves struggles between self and other, embodiment and disembodiment, agency, and passivity, speech, and silence. This view of closure as a strategic, sense-making process suggests that it not only cannot but should not be exorcised from contemporary culture. (Madeira 2012, xxiii)

The Cambridge Dictionary now defines closure in two ways: "Closure, noun (stopping): the fact of a business, organization, etc. stopping operating," and "Closure, noun (emotional): the feeling or act of bringing an unpleasant situation, time, or experience to an end, so that you are able to start new activities. Ex., a sense of closure, to achieve/reach closure" (2023).

Closure has become a societal belief. It has crept into our societal norms and there are hundreds of blogs, books, and articles that further this mythical state of being as an attainable emotional state. It is everywhere. It is not limited to death, tragedy, and trauma. It encompasses divorce, all break-ups, family squabbles, getting fired from a job, and simple arguments in social settings. There are hashtags on social media platforms alerting the world that an individual is trying to find #closure. It has become an expectation.

Closure has also become a lucrative business concept. The funeral industry benefits most by selling the concept of closure, but as traditional funerals and burials have transitioned to cremation and more personal rituals, the industry has had to pivot to more of an event-planning model. Celebrations of life now include slide shows and pop music, and expensive coffins have been replaced by decorative urns. Through these transitions, the price tag has not dropped: the average funeral in the US is $7,848 for burial or $6,971 for cremation. These prices do not include higher-end caskets, flowers, headstones, urns, or ceremonies. The National Funeral Directors of America website states that in 2021, the industry generated $16,323 billion in revenue (NFDA). There is profit to be made in marketing closure.

If we could all see the effects we have on one another, would we make decisions differently? If Timothy McVeigh could have known how deeply he left a mark on the lifeline of a country, would he have made a different choice? The world wanted closure after Oklahoma City only because someone said it was possible. Families wanted closure and the legal system marketed it to them, but in truth they sought an equal level of revenge for the pain he had caused.

If my uncle could have seen the legacy of his death and how profoundly it affected his entire family, would he have welcomed his wife and baby home that fall morning? My family didn't know about closure until someone told us it's why everything still felt stuck. It surely couldn't have come from the fact that no one had ever talked about my uncle's suicide. We never processed, discussed, or had the opportunity to share the truth of our grief. It's been fifty years since he died, and we are all still affected by grief that is intimately our own.

Our lifelines all have a matching mark from that horrible day.

CHAPTER 4

THE WEIGHT OF CARING

TW: Death of a Child

Anyone who is called into the medical field has a deep desire to help. After years of working in many different positions within the medical community, I now care for others in a different way, but my desire to help has never wavered. At times, I care too much.

My medical training gave me incredible career opportunities, and the wisdom from my diverse training has influenced my work as an intuitive medium. It has given me a wider lens to see the totality of my client's issues. There are others who exclusively offer medical medium sessions, but it is only a sliver of what I experience intuitively. During sessions with my clients, there are times I sense scars, old fractures, inflammation, or imbalances. I also sense grief and emotional trauma retained in the energetic field. I discuss what I am sensing with my client and if it needs to be addressed, I recommend they seek care from their physician or medical care practitioner.

Embracing my empathic self, as well as my intuitive abilities, has made me aware how much negative energy I have taken on from patients and colleagues in the past. I was a sponge for toxic energy. I am now very deliberate in protecting my personal boundaries when working with clients. It is a delicate balance to have compassion, to guide with love and care, and to let go of anything that is not mine to carry.

I remain passionate about supporting nurses, doctors, and caregivers who actively work in healthcare. Recently, I was reminded of my own deep emotional scars from my time as an ICU nurse. I was talking with my friend Laurie, who was an administrator at a private college that offers medical education programs. During our conversation, Laurie shared her desire to change the way healthcare professionals are educated and their mental and emotional health honored as both students and professionals.

I agreed that though mental health services currently available to those in the medical field have improved, more could be done.

As we were chatting Laurie asked, "If you had it to do all over again, would you go into nursing again?"

"Yes, absolutely. I loved so many things about being a nurse, but I felt like it took away as much as it gave me," I explained. "The long hours and intense situations are draining, and your family is left with a worn-out shell at the end of the day. The years I worked in the ICU were the most challenging. I'm sure like most nurses, I carry some deep scars from those very special patients. There's one little boy that I will never forget." My voice cracked as I spoke and tears came to my eyes, "I still feel the weight of him. It's a feeling that has never faded thirty years later."

"It must have been really traumatic for you?" Laurie replied, surprised by my tears.

I explained that I had cared for a little boy, a normal toddler just before his second birthday. He had been running and playing and had a freak accident and injured his throat. He ended up in the ICU on a ventilator and eventually suffered brain death. I worked twelve hour shifts back then and I was his nurse for the last three days of his life.

"I can't imagine how hard that must have been. I have grandkids that age now. I don't know how we would have gotten through something like that," Laurie said.

"I cared for his family as much as I cared for him. He looked perfect, like a sweet little boy just taking a nap. There were no outward signs of his injuries, but inside he was dying. It was endless hours of tears as I helped hold all the tubes so his family could hold him as we moved him in and out of the metal crib. I did everything I could to make their time together the best it could be. We all hoped for a miracle, but it never came," I continued.

"There was nothing that could be done to save him?" Laurie asked. "Did they try surgery?"

The doctors declared him brain dead and eventually the family agreed to donate his organs and let him go. I sat with them and answered questions while they made the decision. Then I helped his mom cut locks of his sandy brown hair to keep for herself inside of a locket. It was absolutely heartbreaking. When the time finally came, his mom asked me to stay with him till the end. He had a quilt his grandmother had made for him with one silky peach-colored square at the corner. He liked to rub that square between his fingers, and mom insisted I keep him covered with the quilt until he got into surgery. That one peach square of fabric is etched into my soul.

"I went with the transplant team to the OR, and when I lifted him from the crib into the anesthesiologist's arms, I felt like I was handing him my own child. I had bonded so deeply with him and his family during those three days, and it broke my heart. I still feel the weight of him in my arms."

"I can't imagine how you were able to do that," Laurie said now in tears herself.

"Walking back to the ICU from the surgery department, I was an absolute emotional wreck. I was trying to pull myself together when the charge nurse informed me I was needed for an admission. I know she felt horrible too—everyone working on our unit during those three days was heartbroken by that little boy and his family—but there was another critically ill person coming to take that empty room. I had no time between patients to process or grieve because I had to do my job. Compartmentalize and keep working."

"That seems barbaric. You never got any time to process your emotions? You never got closure," Laurie said compassionately.

Thirty years ago, there were no bereavement classes or opportunities to talk about their emotions after a difficult patient experience. The hospital chaplain was typically the only adjunct staff around at the time of a patient death, but only at the family's request. There was limited support for the mental health of the nurses or medical team, and we all soldiered through it. That experience changed me.

"If you would have gotten some time to process your grief, perhaps it wouldn't still be so emotional for you now." Laurie said.

I explained that I no longer believe that closure is an attainable state of being. I believe deep connections and losses that happen when we work with people in the most intimate moments of their lives have much more impact than we realize. Anyone in the medical field can and will love certain patients, even if it's for a short time, and that love changes us. It is not always easy or positive, and sometimes it's awful, but like anything worth experiencing, it allows us to learn on a soul level.

"What can be done? How can we make those losses less painful so medical staff can remain emotionally supported in their jobs?" Laurie asked.

"I don't have all the answers, but I know we must allow anyone in a caretaking role time to decompress and grieve.

Compartmentalizing is a survival mechanism and eventually we run out of compartments," I answered. I believe healing strategies like movement, yoga, meditation, and therapy have tremendous value. I also think an employer should provide them free of cost, but I am a radical idealist.

The medical community must take care of its own and it is my hope that those who are now suffering from burnout, PTSD, and depression because of the covid years receive the mental health support they deserve. This generation of healthcare workers have been through something that will be documented in history books. The weight of caring has been heavy, and we must ensure we share that burden with those who are hurting.

Experiencing a global pandemic as an intuitive medium and a nurse has also been a life-changing experience. My husband is a doctor, and many of my friends and family are nurses who worked on the front lines of patient care. I felt constant fear for their safety. The uncertainty and distrust in the collective consciousness was palpable for months. The vitriol over masks reminded me of the 1980s when "universal precautions" became a healthcare standard. Some found the simple act of wearing gloves while drawing blood or starting an IV offensive. As a nurse during that time, I received verbal abuse from patients for following newly implemented measures that protected both the patient and the staff. They used homophobic slurs and became angry at the mere insinuation that their bodily fluids may contain any type of virus or pathogen.

The lack of knowledge, rampant homophobia, and the fear surrounding HIV/AIDS affected the world and the entire landscape of healthcare. COVID-19 has done the same. The medical staff who cared for the first waves of COVID-19 patients have undoubtedly been changed by the extreme circumstances they had to battle through. In the first months of the pandemic, we were all in survival mode. That fear and uncertainty has changed us as a society. Though it has become less of a threat, COVID-19 is still with us and will continue to teach us, just as the HIV virus did in the past.

During the pandemic, hundreds of souls left this earth-plane in a very short time and there were moments I would physically experience grief as many souls left their bodies, alone and fearful. Waves of energy would hit me like a tsunami.

There are still times I feel the lurking energy of COVID-19 or the next sophisticated virus waiting to change the human population again. I would be naive to think that the cycles of Mother Nature will not happen as it has for millions of years.

My conversation with Laurie brought back painful memories, but it also reminded me that I am a human having my own complex experience and I have wounds like everyone else. I am grateful to have worked in the medical field and it still offers me a way to be of service today. Emotional pain and energetic wounds must be acknowledged before they can be soothed, and my intuitive abilities allow for that to happen.

CHAPTER 5

WATER CHANGED ME

TW: Natural Disaster, PTSD, Depression

If you stand on a mountain and look down on a river it appears alive and flowing.

As the heavy winter snow melts downward, that river transforms. It looks like a giant snake as it writhes and rolls along rocks and ridges: prehistoric, fearless, and hungry.

With its jaws wide open, it will glutinously drink the water that cascades down from the mountain until it becomes so full and unfamiliar with its own rapidly expanding girth that it screams in pain. Within its churning belly, giant boulders of ice are hurled against one another, crashing and tearing through jammed narrows. Too much and too full, it writhes and fights, it searches for a place to empty itself of churning brown water and debris. It has no choice but to rupture its violent skin and burst through once-sturdy shores. It will heave its fury up onto the land in search of a place to empty out its filthy guts and it will destroy anything that gets in its way. Once the river has emptied its liquid intestines of trees and silt and dank water, it will rest until it finds the energy to slither again. It will slowly begin to find its way back to old sandy bottoms and it will begin to flow again. But not until its damn good and ready.

On March 16, 2019, the Platte River crested at forty feet deep. A river normally shallow enough to wade across was at its deepest level in a hundred years. The once-lazy river had become a sea of broiling muddy water, filled with massive chunks of ice. The frozen boulders banged against one another with the force of a locomotive and the crashing sounds of the ice breaking had been deafening as Mother Nature's fury made herself known.

I had been obsessively monitoring the water levels for weeks, walking up and down the road along the levy south of our development and checking the National Water Service hydrographs online. The rapidly rising water levels had been ominous, and we had been warned that flooding was likely. We had worked diligently to prepare the house by moving valuables to the highest points that we believed to be safe, but on March 15th, we were notified that we had to evacuate. We packed up our two dogs, Dixie and Cooper, and left, not knowing what would be left of our life.

On March 16th, our worst fears became a reality as the Platte River sprawled over its banks and flooded miles of eastern Nebraska, including our lake development. Our ranch-style home sat between the Platte River and a lake. The rear of the house faced the lake and the lower level had multiple sets of French doors that opened onto a patio and sandy beach. Entire kitchens and living areas sat on both floors, but we spent most of our time on the lower level during the summer. The lake had been an idyllic place to live for the prior two years, but when the river flooded, our tranquil lake became a hellish bathtub filled with foul, stagnant water. We could do nothing but wait.

Twenty-four hours after the river overflowed, we were finally allowed to return to assess the damage. Our picturesque development looked like a war zone. Humvees and armed National Guardsmen blocked entry roads to the lake and required identification from anyone entering to protect our homes from looters. As we drove onto our street, the wreckage of the flooding was visible for the first time. Deck furniture was pushed up onto lawns, docks were unmoored and floating randomly, untethered in the lake, and downed trees and debris were everywhere. It was surreal.

The moment we walked through our front door, we were hit by the sound of running water. We ran frantically to every bathroom, making sure the pipes hadn't burst from the cold temperatures, but the upper level was dry. We went to the top of the basement steps and looked down into the lower level now filled with chest-deep water. The water in the basement was moving. It had a current and we could hear furniture bobbing and banging against walls. The sound of running water wasn't a burst pipe. It was the force of the brown water from the lake pouring in through the windows and walls.

We were fortunate that our main level was dry, but the lower level was a fishbowl. We watched as our refrigerator bobbed on its side and bumped into walls and cabinets. We had stacked furniture from the lower-level living and bedroom areas and moved smaller items onto the counter tops in the kitchen. The entire space had looked like a crazy Jenga tower, but we had tried to prevent our things from getting wet. Our efforts had been futile as the force of the water had toppled our well-intended towers.

In those first moments, our minds struggled to process reality. Then our thinking switched to problem solving and the questions came rapid fire. How long can a house sit in four feet of water before it damages the structural integrity? How do you get ahold of FEMA? Will electrical wiring rust? Why does flood water smell so horrible? Does anyone we know have chest waders? Is there sewage in this water? What can we salvage from this mess? Will we ever be able to live here again?

I cried as I tried to process the reality that a significant part of my life was in ruins. Within minutes, my fear became rage. Anger is my default emotion when I'm stressed and Tough Girl from western Nebraska emerges. It only takes seconds for me to become as mean as a rattlesnake. How will we ever be able to live here again? Why did we buy a house by this fucking river? I never wanted this house by this fucking river and I should have listened to my instincts when I asked about the possibility of flooding, but I didn't.

We gathered what we could and tried to secure what was left. The electric panel in the basement was submerged and the main transformers had been shut off to the development. Our home was dark and dangerous. We packed a few more personal things and faced the reality that we couldn't live here and we had no idea when we would be able to again.

As we left that day, we were able to see the immensity of the water's force. The river had rolled through our neighbor's homes, consuming both floors of two-story houses and some only had access to their front door by boat. We felt lucky we had one story that had been saved, but we remained flood refugees.

Those first days were a blur. We made the few decisions we could that gave us a sense of autonomy. We moved in with my son and his wife, who had only been married for three months. Their house was very close to my husband's office, so we felt it would make life easier. We had our dogs and two suitcases for each of us as we cocooned ourselves in their guest bedroom. Uncertainty consumed our days and our nights.

Four days into the disaster, I walked into the front door of my son's split entry house, my arms full of bags, and fell down the steps into the basement and broke my left arm. It was a fracture to my radial head, one of the bones that is important for the arm to bend. It wasn't a bad fracture as fractures go, but it added one more unneeded complication. Luckily, I didn't need a cast and only a sling, but it swelled and throbbed constantly, making it impossible to dress myself and do many basic things. The universe had literally tied my hand to my body, forcing me to ask for help, which is completely out of my comfort zone. I am the person who saves people and fixes things. It was just one more layer of trauma.

Every evening, we went to check the house and monitor the damage. After putting in a full day at the clinic where he works as a family physician, my husband Ryan would put on chest waders and descend the stairs into the chest-deep water. He had moved boxes and valuables to the highest shelves in our storage area, but the force of the water had moved objects and damaged shelves.

He spent hours reaching down into the freezing-cold water to salvage what he could, hoping to save some of our belongings. He was exhausted and stressed. When he finished, he would have to help his broken wife in and out of clothes and pajamas. My husband was pushed to his physical and emotional limits.

After five days of rancid water standing in our house, massive pumps were brought in to drain water from the lake. The water level in our house slowly began to drop so we reached out to friends and family, asking for help. When the water level was finally down to twelve inches, we put out the call. A mass of kind friends and family members arrived with rubber boots, gloves, and hundreds of black, construction-grade trash bags.

"Thank you for coming," I said to everyone as they arrived. It took everything I had to not burst into tears as more volunteers arrived. The support we were given was astonishing. We were grateful and simultaneously wrecked as our friends selflessly waded into the frigid, muddy water.

Pieces of our lives began to emerge from under the water, covered in mud and river silt. Christmas decorations, family pictures, and vintage pieces of bone china were strewn across the front lawn to dry and assess. Most were destroyed by the days in the water and needed to be thrown away. Our losses were material things, but they mattered to us.

Everyone volunteering commented on the smell of the water: "How will you ever get rid of that smell? Is there a chemical or something they can use to get rid of that smell? Hopefully the lake smells better after the water levels go down." The flood water had a unique smell that wasn't exactly must, dead fish, sulfur, or raw sewage, but it was a dank combination of all that hung in the back of your sinuses. It was unfamiliar and intrusive to the senses, and it is a smell that still haunts me.

After five weeks of dealing with our insurance company, FEMA, contractors, and the backlog of our county's bureaucracy, we were able to move back into our house. The basement was a skeleton of bare 4x4s and newly installed electrical wires, but we had heat, electricity, and plumbing. It was a huge relief to no longer be homeless and relying on the generosity of others for a place to stay. Each time some part of our house was brought back to life felt momentous.

After we cooked our first meal in our kitchen, we both sat at our table and wept. Everything appeared to be better from the outside, but the dark tangles of PTSD and depression had taken root.

We were different and we both handled the lasting trauma of the flood differently. My husband went to work each day and spent time away from the house. I was forced to stay there and feel the residual energetic assault. I watched the health of my elderly neighbors decline from the stress of the flood and mourned the passing of our friend John, who lived next door. We were all trying to rebuild our lives, and for many it was too much. Several elderly residents never came back after the evacuation.

Summer came and life moved on. Other families on the lake had the audacity to have Memorial Day celebrations. They had cookouts and pulled skiers across water that was treacherous only two months prior. They laughed and lived as though March had never happened. I hated them. I didn't want to be anywhere near the water. It smelled wrong, different, tainted by sewage and the debris that had flowed over the banks of the river. I didn't trust the water. I will never trust water again.

Obsessively, I continued to check the National Weather Service hydrometer daily. The water levels were low, and the risk was long past, but I couldn't let it go. My broken arm healed and outwardly everything looked fine, but I cried every day. I grieved and I raged. I had insomnia and when I did sleep, my dreams were horrific nightmares. I regretted our decision to move to the lake. I questioned every decision I had ever made.

I stopped doing intuitive work. I felt completely shut down. I had nothing to give, and I doubted I would ever do another reading again. In the years leading up to the flood, I was joyfully absorbed in a life of fairy dust and mysticism. I was a shiny, glittering, radiant spirit who happened to be encumbered by a human body. After the flood, I felt none of that. My light was dimmed. My glitter had been washed away by the water. There was no essential oil or crystal that could have saved us from the devastation of a national disaster. I had to face the truth: We are simply humans at the mercy of Mother Nature.

Throughout the summer our basement remained empty. We wanted the structure to dry completely before we rebuilt. Our washer and dryer were lost to the flood so once a week, I drove to a disheveled laundromat called Laundryville. There I found a warm, quiet cocoon where I could sit and write to the rhythmic tumble of warm dryers. It was during my weekly wash-and-fold routine that I met other survivors of the flood. They wore the same hollow-eyed expression of exhaustion that I recognized in my own face when I looked in the mirror. Week after week, they drug in their huge, black garbage bags filled with unmistakable, musty laundry they had salvaged from the water.

We had tearful conversations as our clothes tumbled dry, and I was grateful to know that there were others who were struggling with the trauma left by the flood. I held babies as their mother's folded clothes, and we talked about the challenges of being displaced and at the mercy of friends and family. Many would never be able to return to their homes again. The water had destroyed their houses completely.

I wrote about the characters that emerged at Laundryville and my blogs were a way to share what we were experiencing. *Letters from Laundryville* became my catharsis and helped me to reconnect with my creative mind. Writing through my feelings was healing to my soul.

Laundryville was falling apart a little more each week. The last day I spent there felt like walking into a crime scene. A number of the machines had "Out of Order" stickers pasted on them, and a stream of water ran from under one of the washers all the way through the center of the building. Seriously, another damn flood? Laundryville was no longer just shabby. It was officially becoming dangerous. It had been a place of solace for me, and when it finally closed, I cried as though I had lost an old friend.

Many of our neighbors whose homes were also damaged by the flood water had rushed to rebuild in the restoration of their houses. The structures hadn't dried sufficiently so they were dealing with the consequence of mold and rot. We had allowed our basement to fully dry for six months, and when we felt that mold was no longer a risk, we began to rebuild. Friends had long stopped asking how we were doing. Our disaster had been a blip on their radar, and as construction began, everyone assumed that life was back to normal.

"Wow, you're getting a great new basement out of the deal. You must be so excited," my friend Jacque said one morning over coffee. She probably didn't mean to be so flippant, but the insensitivity of humans is astounding. "Have you figured out paint colors and flooring?"

"Well, it's not exactly a remodel. It's been more of salvage and restore for us," I answered sharply. I had met my friend for coffee not because I wanted to but because I needed to do normal things and get back into some kind of routine.

"I'm sure it will really elevate your home value. I know when we updated our basement, it really improved the value…" she continued her ridiculous, selfish bullshit.

As she was talking, a wave of heat rolled through me. My mind shut down and I stopped listening. It took every bit of my strength to hold back the rage that was boiling inside of me. She didn't know that I wanted to stand up and tell her to fuck off.

"Who gives a shit about your basement, Jacque?" I screamed inside my head.

It had taken a massive amount of effort for me to be there in the first place and now all I wanted to do was run away. I regretted coming and subjecting myself to trivial conversations that felt empty and meaningless. But isn't this what humans are supposed to be doing? Interacting and sharing experiences? Talking about the mundane happenings of life. Isn't that what I loved to do before the flood? I loved to talk, share, and be social. I had changed and at that moment I was miserable. All I wanted to do was to go home and curl up and cry.

For months I self-isolated and avoided people. I knew I wasn't okay, so I went back to my tried-and-true self-help strategies like gratitude lists and journaling, but I could never seem to find the right mantra or meditation to lift me from my funk. I gathered my crystals and asked my spirit guides to give me strength and direction, but I heard a message that I hadn't heard in years.

"First, heal thyself."

There was no getting over or around it. I was grieving and it was going to take time.

In November 2019, the restoration and rebuilding of the lower level of our house was complete. The house felt normal again and getting past all that comes with having contractors in our space was a relief. I began to feel hopeful again. We thought 2020 was to be a better year for us, but as my husband and I clinked flutes of champagne together on New Year's Eve, we had no idea of what was just around the corner.

In February, the news channels reported that the Platte River was rising again and there was a good chance of flooding. The evening news began showing clips of low-level flooding to the north of Omaha, and every time I saw it, it sent me into panic attacks. My heart raced, I would cry uncontrollably, and I had nightmares about the water and drowning. The thought of going through another flood consumed me. I repeatedly checked the weather service river hydrometers, praying we would be spared of a second disaster.

During this same time, there were inklings of a virus that was spreading in China. As a physician, my husband kept us abreast of the data the CDC was reporting. At that time, they believed we were at minimal risk and had nothing to fear. Both our children were expecting their first babies that spring. They were due in the first part of May, and we were looking forward to their births. We had no idea that our grandchildren would be born during the first wave of the COVID-19 pandemic.

The water levels in the Platte River were high, but not like the previous spring and we were spared of a second flood. We had the chaos of COVID-19 pandemic instead. I'm sure that surviving both a flood and a pandemic simultaneously would have been my undoing. Our guardian angels had saved us from another heartbreak.

My grandchildren were born three weeks apart in May of 2020. The unbridled love I felt for them broke me open again. Because of all the uncertainty and chaos around COVID-19, I agreed to care for them during the day while their parents worked. Those beautiful babies gave me a purpose, and caring for them saved me mentally during those months of isolation.

Through the months of the pandemic lockdown, I surfed www.Realtor.com, my architectural porn. It was a harmless diversion from reality. I mindlessly looked at bedrooms, and window treatments, and bemoaned the overuse of gray paint. I dreamed of having a second home in a town far away from the water, but I was sure no one would ever buy a lake house so close to the Platte River that had flooded the previous year.

In August of 2020, as my husband was recovering from hernia surgery, I noticed a listing for a gorgeous red-brick mansion on a highly sought-after street in Omaha. I had always dreamed of living in that historic neighborhood, but the home prices had always seemed unattainable. I was intrigued, and a bit baffled, when I looked at the price. It was in our price range. As I opened the pictures and saw the black-and-white checkered floor and the oak staircase in the entryway, I just knew. I looked through the rest of the pictures, and for the first time in a long time, I was excited about a house.

I took my iPad out to the couch where my husband was resting after hernia surgery earlier that week.

"Pack your shit; we are moving."

"What?" he answered, groggy from pain medication.

"Look at this house. It's amazing. It's ridiculous and huge, and amazing," I answered as I handed him my iPad so he could see the listing.

"Wow, it's incredible. We should go look at it," he said as he scrolled through the online pictures.

"I've already texted Beth. We are going on Friday," I said.

"Okay, well I hope I'm feeling better by then," he said as he adjusted the ice bags over his newly healing incisions.

"I think it's on one of the highest points in the city. It can't flood. I know this all sounds crazy, but it looks amazing." I knew this was going to be our house. I felt guided in a way that I hadn't in a long time.

After touring the gorgeous old mansion, we made an offer and the sellers accepted. In spite of our doubts, we sold our lake house in one day. It was a huge relief to be able to let go of that constant fear and worry. We could feel safe again.

Moving in the middle of a pandemic was stressful, but after dealing with the flood, the move was well worth the effort. Relocating helped my mental health. I didn't have to look out my door and see water every day.

There are still times when I see or smell reminders of the flood and I have a visceral reaction. On a recent vacation with my girlfriends, we arrived in North Carolina during heavy rain and flood warnings. Our Airbnb house was a quaint A-frame in a remote forest and the roads were muddy and difficult when we arrived. Every raindrop on the metal roof of the house was a poke in the shoulder from my PTSD. I didn't sleep and I didn't relax until the sky cleared and I knew we were out of danger.

I weep with empathy for survivors during news stories and reporting of national disasters. My PTSD is still a part of me that I am learning to work with. It's no longer my enemy, but more like a bitchy cousin I have to tolerate at family gatherings. I don't like her, but we are in this for the long haul.

I have grieved the me that lived before the flood, and now I have the lived experience of integrating my own fear and loss into my psyche. If my life has its own seismogram, there is a deep cleave where the flood impacted my lifeline, but bit by bit, I have found my way back to trusting my intuitive abilities. I am lovingly working with clients again. I am more empathetic and understanding in my intuitive work and my grief has deepened my connection with Spirit. I wish there was a magic bullet or perfect crystal that could create a sense of closure and allow us to skip through all the emotions that come with trauma, but I know with absolute certainty that closure is a lie.

CHAPTER 6

YOU'RE A WHAT? THE WORK OF AN INTUITIVE MEDIUM

When I introduce myself to strangers as an intuitive medium, the response is typical: "You're a what?"

It's not a common line of work and always requires an explanation about mediumship. Then the curiosity of the newly acquainted takes over.

"Do you see anyone dead around me?"
"Is this place haunted?"
"So, are you a Christian?"
"Am I ever going to be rich?"

The skeptics, the believers, the non-believers, and the religiously devout all react very similarly. Being in the presence of psychics and mediums brings about immediate curiosity and a giddy, adolescent sort of "truth or dare" energy to first impressions. Glimpsing a mystical realm or accessing souls on the other side is a bit like having the key to a secret world. The curiosity is tantalizing.

The path from connecting with my intuitive abilities to becoming a professional intuitive medium who charges for services unfolded slowly, and a million magical things happened along the way. I didn't leave the Panera Bread after doing my first reading and set up a folding table on the sidewalk with a sign selling my services. I took things very, very slowly.

I began offering readings as practice for friends or students at my yoga studio and it was simply an exchange of energy. Those initial readings gave me confidence and always brought a sense of joy and wonder. I could channel names, dates, stories, and information and when we finished a session, I was as amazed as my client. I felt euphoric after readings.

After several months of free sessions, I finally got the courage to begin charging for my work. It was a monumental step for me because I don't like asking for anything and deciding what to charge for my not-so-traditional service made me very uncomfortable. It also meant I would have to create a website and a payment system, which meant I had to own my title. I couldn't lurk around in the world like a little forest fairy, popping from one flower to the next. I had to be accountable. Ugh!

During the first years of intuitive work, I was willing to do readings anywhere. Group gatherings, boutique open houses, bachelorette parties, and company Christmas parties. You name it, my table was set up and my cards and crystals were at the ready. It was fun and extremely challenging. Doing ten consecutive readings is very draining and I learned very quickly to practice very strong energetic boundaries. If I didn't create a giant bubble of energy around myself, I would feel hungover and have an intense migraine the day after. It was a hard lesson learned.

Those first years were the foundation for my work today. My clients have always come from referrals. A friend who met me at a gallery opening gives my name to her friend and so on. It is a lovely strand of healing and friendship that has woven some incredible connections over the years. I have clients all over the globe, and I have provided readings for thousands of beautiful human beings. It has been an incredible journey.

My practice with clients and my sessions has changed very little over time. For over a decade, I have created a routine and a flow that works well for me. It might not be the right fit for others, but my clients and I both feel nurtured and supported in my sessions and that is all that matters.

I start everyday by meditating and I set at an intention. I ask Spirit to guide me and for the greatest good to come from any of the work that I do. I ask that any and all energy that I encounter be used in the most loving way. I follow my intentions with gratitude, and I let go of any need to control the outcomes of my sessions. Letting go of my ego's need to get it perfect has come with practice, but I'm still human and I love it when my readings are super-duper amazing.

Usually during my morning meditation, images or bits of information start to appear. Those images are almost always for the clients I will see later that day. It's like bits of colored glass or short clips of a movie that individually make no sense. I allow myself to see or feel them briefly and then let them go. I trust that they will emerge again in our session if they are important when the time comes.

"I see huge bras. I've been seeing them all day. Big white bras with four or five snaps in the back," I said during a session with my client, Carrie.

"Bras. Hmm. That is strange. It's not making any sense to me," she replied curiously.

"There is a woman with very large breasts, and she is complaining about these huge bras. She said it was such a burden, but you helped her get those bras on even when she wasn't very nice to you," I explained as the flow of conversation began to open more from the spirit of an older woman I had connected with.

"That's my mom," Carrie replied as tears came to her eyes. "She was a very difficult person to be around in her later years, but I helped her as much as I could. And she had huge boobs and giant bras."

I laughed and shook my head, "I never know what will happen in a reading, and I don't choose the things to come through in readings, but we just have to roll with it."

Our session continued, and I shared the information that came through from her mother and other spirits that wished to send her a message. I talked about her grief and some personal energetic wounds that needed attention, and I also allowed her to acknowledge her own intuitive abilities. I encouraged her to nurture those abilities. A reading that started with bras became a soul connection and after our session we became friends. Carrie and I have shared several adventures together, including a trip to Spain where I co-led a women's retreat. I adore her.

Each intuitive session is different. I open myself up as a channel, and whatever emerges is unique. A hot rush or a feeling of a wave of energy rolls through me, and then images begin to appear in my mind's eye. It's a bit like remembering a movie I have watched in the past. I see moving images in my mind. It is fleeting, and sometimes there is dialogue. There are some who can see spirits, like the boy in the movie *Sixth Sense*, but my experience is a bit different. When people ask if I can see dead people, the answer is sometimes. Mostly, I feel and hear them.

During my sessions, I feel my client's energetic field. I feel their pain, past traumas, grief, love, and issues that they may have not realized were still affecting their life. I also see numbers, and those are typically connected with their lifeline or marks on their personal seismogram. Many times, these marks or events form an energetic loop that keeps bringing us back to the same feeling or problem over and over again. If the number seventeen pops into my mind, it is probably a pattern of big life events that happen every seventeen years. I call them "transition years." Having awareness of these loops or "transition years" gives us the opportunity to prepare or become aware that wonderful changes may be in store for us. It's just one more tool in the toolbox of life.

People often ask if I read everyone, or if I am sensing spirits everywhere I go. The answer is no. I have a very hard and fast rule that when I am off the clock, I am off the clock. I shut down the channel and I go about my normal daily life. I get signs or spirit nudges, just like everyone else, but I try not to overanalyze or give meaning to things that are just random happenings in life. Some buildings or people feel uncomfortable or off-putting to me energetically, and I allow myself to feel that sensation, acknowledge it, and then, if possible, leave the situation. I do my best to avoid returning.

I do believe a feather on your path is a message from your angels, and cardinals are a hello from a loved one who have passed. Signs come in many lovely ways. The risk in assigning meaning is that we start to overthink everything. Clients will reach out and ask what it means if a cat ran in front of their car or a bird died on their lawn. Most of the time, a dead bird is just a bird that met the end of its life, and cats make bad traffic decisions daily.

"What does it mean to you?" I asked my client Joel, who had been seeing the numbers eleven-eleven repeatedly.

"It grabs my attention. I see it everywhere I go. I feel like I am supposed to be doing something, but I don't know what that is," Joel answered.

"Repeating numbers can be messages from our angels, or Spirit, but most importantly, when it happens try to notice what you feel in the moment. Are you stressed? Did you just think of someone? Does it make you want to reach out to someone? Allow the energy of the experience to tell you what the message is and trust it. Google is a good place to get information, but your own intuition is far better," I explained.

It took years for me to trust my own intuition, and I believe anyone can become more skilled in their personal psychic abilities. It takes time and practice, like any other art of ability. Trusting it is the hard part.

The most challenging part of my work is holding space for clients who are sad or grieving every day. My clients want answers, they want an end to their pain, and they are seeking the mythical properties of closure. I do what I can to provide answers that will give them a sense of peace.

I am often asked what it is like on the other side and what happens to our soul when we die. I believe when we leave our physical body, our soul exists in a complete form, even grander and vaster than we can imagine. We transition to a different plane of existence, and our spirit lives on infinitely. We may call it heaven, the cosmos, another dimension, or our soul's home, but we are joyfully received by loved ones upon our arrival. The love and connection we experienced as humans continues after our physical passing, and we are more present, capable, and willing to help those who remain on this earth plane. We are pure love.

At times, my own grief and emotional healing have needed to be my priority, and my intuitive self-had to be put aside. After the flood, and after the death of a close friend, I have taken necessary breaks from intuitive work. I honored those times by letting myself feel my sadness and process my grief in my own way. I didn't make announcements or take down my website. I let Spirit do the work for me. Clients stopped calling and referrals seemed to be suspended in time, and then slowly as I healed and came out of my cocoon, the requests for readings resumed.

Taking my own advice is tough and I'm frequently my own worst client, but if we allow ourselves to be guided by Spirit, everything works itself out in divine timing.

Over the years, I have worked with hundreds of clients, and it remains an honor and privilege. It has been a long and winding road, full of obstacles and challenges, but my intentions have never changed. I hold my clients in the highest regard and trust that all energy is shared for the greater good. If I can shift the sadness in one heart, it will have a ripple effect that can shift a million others. That sustains me when the going gets tough.

PART II

THEIR STORIES

Part 2 is a journey through the stories of my clients as an intuitive medium. Each of these powerful and inspiring stories captures the profound impact that our loved ones have on our lives, even after they have passed on. Through my intuitive gifts, I was able to connect with the spiritual realm and provide my clients with a sense of comfort and healing and dispel the myth of closure. Join me as we explore the depth and beauty of the human experience, and the connections that transcend our physical world.

These chapters contain topics which may be difficult to read or triggering, including the death of a child, death of a parent, suicide, depression, post-traumatic stress disorder, infant loss, and divorce.

CHAPTER 7

DREW AND KATHERINE

TW: Death of a Child

I had been preparing myself for the clients who were to arrive at any second. They had scheduled an intuitive reading two weeks prior, and I had no information about them other than a first name. But before they arrived, I could begin to sense their anxiety. My hands felt tingly, my stomach had butterflies and, in my mind, pictures were darting in and out. I had meditated that morning and moved through the same routine I have had for years: meditation, setting intentions, and declaring to the universe that any work done with clients be for the highest and best good. My heart sped up as the doorbell rang. This session was going to be intense.

Drew was a tall, middle-aged man with sandy blond hair that was thinning on top. He wore a yellow polo shirt and gray golf shorts, looking as though he had just finished eighteen holes at a country club. His wife, Katherine, was a beautiful brunette with dark brown eyes and a petite frame. She was tan and thin, and wearing white shorts that accentuated her toned legs.

I could feel their apprehension as they sat down on my sofa, both stiff as soldiers.

"Who gave you my name?" I asked, "I always like to thank the person who connected us."

Drew spoke first, "It was actually my doctor. He knew I was struggling with some issues, and he suggested I see a medium. I was surprised at first, but then I thought what the hell. Nothing else has worked, so why not?" Katherine sat silently beside him.

Immediately, as Drew was speaking, I began to feel a hot sensation moving through my body, like standing in front of a giant hand dryer in a public restroom. Images began to pop into my mind, as though I was remembering scenes from a movie. My stomach felt tight, and I felt nauseous. I experienced it from the perspective of someone whose life had ended from something that went very wrong in their stomach, throat, and intestinal system. It felt miserable.

I began to share what I was seeing and feeling. I described the sensations of nausea and the man that was communicating with me. He was large in stature and had a very big personality.

Drew turned and looked at his wife, their eyes widened, and Katherine said, "I have goosebumps. Look at my arms!" She was holding up her forearm in front of Drew and the raised skin on her arm was visible. Her demeanor had changed completely from shy and disconnected to enthralled.

"I feel that this man had major issues with his throat, stomach, and esophagus," I continued. "It was a really hard illness and death, but that's not what he wants you to remember. He's very clearly wanting you to remember a million other things about him, not just those last moments of his life."

There were tears in Drew's eyes, and I could feel his energetic walls starting to come down. Our session began to flow, and we agreed that the man who was sharing his information that day was Drew's father who had recently passed from esophageal and stomach cancer. We talked about his father's sense of humor and his love of hunting.

"Your grief is immense, and it feels as though you have had multiple deaths recently. It's not just your dad," I said as our session continued to unfold. "You have had loss after loss. Oh my goodness, the two of you really have been through it." My heart hurt as I spoke because I could feel the intense grief they were experiencing.

Drew answered, "Yes, we have been through some really tough stuff this past year." He was much more relaxed now and he looked over at Katherine. "I don't know how I would have made it without her."

I could see the two were deeply in love, connected but simultaneously being pulled apart by their grief and sadness. I allowed myself to go deeper, to settle into the energy of the moment, and I began to feel the sensation of a traumatic impact. It felt like I was in an accident and my head was hitting something stationary, like a wall or a pole. There was no time to react; it had happened so quickly. Alive and then gone in one flash. There was no in between. It was as though there was laughter and a conversation, and then within only a few minutes this trauma happened. The soul I had connected with felt completely calm and relaxed. It felt like they had become a cloud: soft, floating, free, and very peaceful.

"It feels like there is someone who died in a traumatic accident," I said, "but when I connect with them now, it's like being a cloud or a puff of smoke. I can't describe it any other way."

Tears were now streaming down both Drew and Katherine's cheeks. I reached for the box of tissues I always keep on a coffee table by the sofa. Tears are usually a part of every session.

As Drew and Katherine wiped their cheeks, I continued to describe the images that were emerging in my mind. "This person was very easy, very relaxed, and at peace. It felt like they had lived their entire life that way, like a surfer dude or a mountain man. Nothing got them riled up or excited. They want me to make sure you know the accident was a fluke. It just happened and no one was to blame. It was a random moment and there was no way it could have been prevented. There's no reason to keep asking everyone who was there to explain it again. It was an accident."

"It was our son. He died a few months ago in a freak accident and we have been completely devastated," Katherine said as her voice cracked with the pain of a mother's grief. "He was with friends. He had one beer, so we know he wasn't drunk, but they were messing around and he fell and hit his head."

Drew leaned forward and put his elbows on his knees, his hands over his face and sobbed into his palms as Katherine spoke. His lanky arms and legs seemed to create a shield for his broken heart as his wife retold the story.

"Are you okay, Drew?" I asked. "We can stop for a minute if you need to." I could feel how intensely he was hurting,

"I'm okay," he responded as he sat back and dropped his hands into his lap. "I just haven't been able to get over this. I was hoping we would find out something today that would give us closure." Katherine reached over and took his hand, lacing their fingers together.

Their grief is heavy and intense. As an empathic and intuitive person, I feel it all the way down into the marrow of my bones. As a mother, I feel their grief on a deeply human level, and I cannot fathom how one goes on after the loss of a child, but my work is now helping those who have, so I continue with our session.

I explained my belief that there is no such thing as closure. It's not a real state of being. I further explained that I can help find some answers, but your grief and sadness are going to be with you forever.

"Your love isn't going to go anywhere, and neither is his. You will remain connected forever. It's the best and worst thing about being a human. Some days will be better than others, but you will always love and miss him. I can't give you closure, but I can give you some help and eventually when you talk about him, it will hurt a little less."

Drew answered through tears, "I don't want to feel this way anymore, but I don't know how else to feel. He was my best friend; we did everything together. We had so many plans and now they are just gone."

The messages were strong, and I was certain they were from his son. "I'm supposed to tell you to do it all. Take the trips, go to the lake, catch the fish, go to the cabin, and he will be there with you. He's around you all the time now. He leaves you signs he's there and you want to see them, but you keep talking yourself out of it. He said you have changed the lightbulb in the lamp where you sit and read several times in the past few weeks because it keeps turning on and off. It's not the bulb. It's him saying hi."

Drew and Katherine looked surprised and began to giggle and cry simultaneously.

"How could you possibly know that?" Drew said in astonishment. "There's no way you could know that! It has been driving me crazy, and I haven't told anyone, so there's no way you could know that. It's him? He's been messing with me. Oh my god, I wanted to believe it was him, but I also don't believe in this kind of stuff, but I had hoped it was him!"

"Yes," I said. "It's definitely him and he's a bit of a prankster. He loves to have fun and the two of you always messed with each other relentlessly." I could feel the playful energy of this lively young man. A picture of a young man in his early twenties was becoming clearer in my mind, like an image in a pool of water through gentle waves. Long curls of sandy blond hair, and broad wide shoulders, his energy loose and soft like a cloud, but emerging more vividly.

"Oh my goodness," said Katherine. "I am in a house full of boys, and they have always picked on each other, but especially Jeff." It was the first time either had spoken his name out loud. "He was the youngest and such a joker. He didn't take anything serious, which drove us a little crazy, but he was so funny. He always made us laugh."

I smiled as I felt the joy of this family emerging. "He wants you to keep laughing and telling stories about the fun times. And your dad wants me to remind you that he was funny too. Your dad told filthy jokes. He wants me to make sure you know that he and Jeff are having a great time together. One of them is also good at card tricks. I can see cards being laid out on a table like a magician in Las Vegas."

"That was my dad," Drew answered. "He loved doing card tricks and entertaining the kids. This is crazy. I don't even know what to say. I had no idea that today would be like this. Is Jeff okay? I just need to know that he's okay."

I answered as the information filtered through from two men sitting at a bar laughing at a joke. They were both relaxed and getting a real kick out of the punch line. "They are together, they are okay, and they are having a laugh. You can stop worrying about them and just let yourself see the signs when they come. When it happens, all you have to do is say hi or thank you. You are the one stuck here in all the human stuff. They are released from this human experience, and they are great."

The session continued as we talked about stories of Jeff, and of Drew's father, and eventually, we ended our time together with a good laugh. A few weeks later, I received a text from Drew thanking me for helping him find his way back to his old self. He was still grieving his son, but finding signs that Jeff was still very near and still playing tricks on him.

My intention is always to help, and when someone walks out of my door, I hope they feel better than when they walked in. I don't have any expectations, but I trust, I listen, and then I let the conversation flow. I also believe what we need will find us when we are ready. There is a way to find a light in the darkness of grief.

CHAPTER 8

GORDON

TW: Divorce

Can you help someone let go of the worst pain of their life?

Gordon was in his late thirties and had been referred by his friend Chris, who had been a client of mine for several years. Gordon had recently gone through a divorce and was struggling with stress and anger.

I could feel his tension during our introductions. He avoided eye contact, and he was reluctant to share much more than his first name and that he was employed as a maintenance person at a factory. His energetic walls were high and extremely thick.

I explained to Gordon that Reiki is an energetic healing method created by Dr. Mikao Usui from Japan. During our session, he would lie down and relax on a massage table as I moved my hands in different positions over his body to allow *chi*, or energy, to flow freely. The discipline of Reiki has been practiced throughout the world since the early 1900s, and

I have been sharing it with clients for many years. "When the Japanese word Reiki is broken down, Reiki means spiritual energy. It can be described as the energy of everything" (Stiene and Stiene 2005, 4).

I feel the universal energy of all humans is love, so when I share Reiki with another, I am a channel of universal love energy to them.

"Okay, I am not sure what that means, but let's do this," Gordon said as he removed his coat and boots and lay down on the massage table.

I began our session by asking for Gordon's consent to receive Reiki and setting an intention. We asked that our angels, spirit guides, and loving energies surrounded our session and brought loving energy to Gordon. I began a deep breathing pattern and allowed myself to ground the energy for both of us. As I moved my hands above his body, I could feel heaviness and a deep sense of loss. His energy felt sticky, as though my hands were moving through thick, marshmallow cream. When I placed my hands above his heart center, it felt as if there was a tornado, swirling and destructive. I continued moving my hands above his body, feeling and assessing all his energy centers.

"Your mind is racing," I said as I moved upward, and I softly placed my hands on each side of his head. It felt as though there was a buzzing under my palms.

"Yea, this feels really strange. No one, other than my kids, has touched me in a long time," he answered.

I felt a shift with those words. As he spoke of his children, I could feel the energy beneath my hands become less prickly to my palms. In my mind, I began to see several children, close in age, running and playing.

"You have quite a few kids. It looks like five."

"Yes, how did you know that?" he asked, perplexed.

"It's what I do. I pick up on things that are important to you or that you are holding within your energetic field," I explained as I moved my hands and placed a Reiki symbol above his third eye chakra at the center of his forehead.

I continued moving my hands through the Reiki positions, and I felt guided to spend some time at his heart center. I pulled up a chair at the head of the table and reached my hands over his shoulders and lightly placed my hands directly onto the center of his chest. Immediately, he began to breathe very deeply. My hands felt like they were being sucked down into a black hole, and then images of his anger and rage appeared in my mind.

"You have been struggling with some anger, but it feels as though it's all coming directly from your heart. It's sucking the life out of you, Gordon," I said gently, as I held my hands very still.

He began to weep. "My wife wanted a divorce. I didn't. It came out of nowhere. I went to work one day and thought everything was fine, but when I got home, she told me she was done." The tears were pouring from his eyes and down the sides of his face. He began to sob, his body lurching with each sob.

I continued to breathe deeply and hold my hands firmly, sending healing energy to his turbulent heart. His sobs became guttural wails, and he released the violent pain from inside his body. It was as though his energy was pushing my hands away for the protection of his wounds. His release was primal and louder than anything I had experienced in a Reiki session, but I held space lovingly for him.

After several minutes, he stopped wailing and his breath slowed. It felt as though a circle of guardian angels came in and hovered above his heart. I sensed warm yellow light beaming down from his guardians through my hands. He became calmer and I felt a shift. The energy of his heart space changed and appeared as a crack or fissure in my mind. I envisioned the image of a man walking along the edge of a deep canyon. "Are you planning to go to the Grand Canyon, or were you there recently?"

"Yes, a couple of months ago I went with some friends and hiked the South Rim. It was the first trip I have taken without my family since the divorce. It was fun, but there were times it broke my heart to be there without them," he answered. "I don't know how to be me without them. I'm a family guy. That's all I know how to do."

I lifted my hands from his heart space and continued through the rest of my hand positions, and then placed the sacred symbols of Reiki throughout the areas of his energetic field. In his heart space, I placed the *Cho Ku Rei* symbol, which sends power to strengthen the areas Gordon felt weakened. I also moved my hands above his body to draw the *Sei He Ki* symbol, which brings balance to his emotions and his masculine and feminine energies.

When the session was complete, I brought him a glass of water and we sat down to talk. He shared his devastation from the divorce. He was struggling with his emotions and had been having angry outbursts at work. He had been warned that if his behavior didn't improve, he would be terminated.

"I have never cried like that," he admitted. "I have been furious and felt betrayed by her, but I have never cried. It felt terrible when it was happening, but I feel better."

"Well, clearly you needed to release a lot of pain. I am grateful you were willing to come for a session and that you were open to it," I said. "I feel like I just wrestled an alligator, but I'm glad you showed up."

"Oh, I almost didn't. If Chris hadn't called me and talked to me on the drive here, I would have turned around and gone home. I had no idea what I was getting into."

We talked about his children and his current state of mind. He had been working out and it showed. His body was very muscular. He had funneled his rage into his workouts and shared that he had hoped if he looked better, perhaps his ex-wife might be attracted to him again. His only desire was to get back together with her, but she had made it clear that was not what she wanted. They had been high school sweethearts and she was the only woman he had ever loved. Their divorce had left him lost and without an identity.

"I don't want to feel like this anymore. I want my old life back," he said. "I still don't know why she quit on us. We were great and then in one day, it was over."

I felt compassion for his sadness and could not feel any sense of infidelity surrounding their divorce. Intuitively, I felt as though the marriage had just come to an end.

"What I have learned after many years of doing this work is that in a break-up there is usually one person who wants the relationship to end and one who does not. The person who has been thinking about leaving experiences a catalyst or a tipping point and finally makes the decision. They have already grieved and begun to move forward. The partner who was left behind is unprepared and hasn't had time to process or move through grief and loss. It's unexpected and, as you have said, it feels like a betrayal."

We talked about how he could let go of his need to win his wife back and allow himself to grieve. I encouraged him to turn his intense feelings toward his children and to funnel his love in ways that could be supportive of them and his ex-wife. His hike in the Grand Canyon had been a major first step and he wanted to be open to other future adventures. He needed to create a new identity for himself as a single man as he grieved the end of his marriage. We also talked about adding a meditation practice to his workout routine and ways to allow his sadness to be released in ways that didn't involve raging at his co-workers.

"Anger, rage, and obsessive behaviors can mask the true source of our pain," I continued. Feeling as though we have been rejected is a hard pill to swallow, no one likes it, but we will all experience it at some time in our lives. Love creates a bond, and we can't un-love someone after we have made that energetic connection. We can only move forward knowing another human has shared our walk through life with us for a time, but we are moving forward on different paths.

After a relationship ends, grief is left over. Whether that grief is for the happily-ever-after fantasy we created in our mind or if it is for the energy required to create a new, independent version of ourselves, breakups are hard. Divorce is the death of a marriage and must be grieved with a similar level of reverence. Unfortunately, that rarely happens and culturally, more focus is given to creating the perfect profile for dating websites than to healing our emotional and energetic selves.

Gordon's tender heart felt warm and calm when we hugged before he left that day. I knew that the loving energy of Reiki was exactly what he needed, and I was grateful he had a friend willing to send him for a session. Holding sacred space is challenging, but it is a calling and with each client, I am grateful to be a channel for love and healing.

CHAPTER 9

MACKENZIE

TW: Pregnancy Loss

Before we take our first breath and enter this life, a million miracles must occur. One egg and one sperm must meet in perfect timing. Cells undergo a process of division and reproduction, and the result is a fully formed individual. At any moment in that process, one shift in one individual cell can change the entire magnificent cascade. Is this all random or are miracles orchestrated from a higher plane of existence? Is our destiny predetermined or is it all unfolding beautifully before us?

On a warm, fall afternoon in September 2012, brown autumn leaves had begun to collect on the sidewalk in front of my studio. The front door opened and a beautiful young woman who looked to be in her late twenties stepped inside. MacKenzie had come to the studio for hypnosis. She had a wide smile, bright blue eyes, and shoulder-length dark brown hair.

I welcomed her, and after she had finished her paperwork, we walked to the hypnosis room at the back of the studio.

The room had a comfortable reclining chair and recording equipment. As she sat down and settled in the recliner, I could sense her nervousness, but I also felt an odd sense of familiarity with MacKenzie.

"Have we met before or did someone refer you? I always like to send out a thank you to anyone who sends me clients," I asked hoping to find out if my intuition was right.

"No, we've never met. My boss, Will, recommended you," MacKenzie answered. "He has told me several times that the two of us needed to meet, and then when I found out you did hypnosis, I decided to reach out. I'm trying to get pregnant, and I want to go into the process super healthy and strong."

Will was an old friend and I assumed that the link we shared must have been the source of my initial feeling. We agreed on the goals for her hypnosis, then we moved through the process of relaxation, suggestions, and re-emergence. After our session, I created a CD and sent her on her way, confident she would get pregnant soon.

Nine months later, MacKenzie returned to our studio. Her physical appearance looked the same, but her energy was completely different. The first time I met MacKenzie, her energy was big and bright, radiating far outside of her physical body with bold color. That day it was barely visible around her and no longer vivid and colorful.

"I have been through a really hard time these last few months," she began as we took our seats in the hypnosis room. "I got pregnant very soon after our first meeting. I was so happy, and things were going perfectly until we got our first ultrasound. The baby had some significant birth defects, and we were told she would need to have intrauterine surgery to survive. We were unsure of her survival in the womb, and then we were told that soon after she was born, she would need a kidney transplant right away." She was remarkably composed as she spoke. "Someone else's baby would have to have died for my baby to live. It was torturous and I felt like those weeks we were in some kind of mental purgatory."

"Oh no, MacKenzie," I answered. "I am so sorry. This must have been horrendous for you."

"It gets worse," she took a deep breath and went on. "When we returned for our next ultrasound, there was no heartbeat. In one single moment, all the decisions we were struggling with were taken away. A few days later, I had to deliver her and let her go. During my delivery, I had an extreme amount of bleeding, and I stopped breathing. I think my body was so traumatized from all the pain of letting her go that I just stopped breathing and drifted away. I was in shock, and I only have little snippets of memory from that day. It was so terrible."

I listened as my heart broke for this young woman and her husband.

"It's been four months since she died. I had to have transfusions after the delivery, which helped, but I have decided I want to try to get pregnant again. I know if I get pregnant again right away, I'll be able to move past this. I want either hypnosis or Reiki again to help get me pregnant again," she answered with a steely determination that seemed a mismatch to the grief that she had just described.

I felt Reiki would be the best way to help MacKenzie, so we proceeded with a session. As I moved my hands above her body, I could feel a dark, heavy, sticky energy in the space over her belly. I explained what I was feeling as I continued and told her she was still in energetic pain. I could see her grief inside my mind's eye as a large rock that was heavy and immovable, like a river rock with water moving around it. I also sensed two huge swords crossed in front of her body as a gesture of protection. Those swords were allowing nothing in or out that might harm her.

After our session, we sat down to review what I had sensed during our Reiki session. "MacKenzie, your body isn't ready to get pregnant again," I said. "You need some time."

She disagreed with me. Her determination was unshakable. She began explaining all the steps she had taken to ensure she was physically ready to conceive another baby.

"Did I mention that I am adopted? I think I told you that. I have contacted both of my birth parents and there are no genetic birth defects that either is aware of. Come to think of it, you might know my birth father. He's in the wellness business too."

"Wait, what? No, you have never mentioned that you were adopted," I said as a huge rush of energy passed through me. At that moment, it was as if a million pieces of a puzzle were coming together there before me. I had seen those same blue eyes many times before. "I know exactly who your dad is. You have his eyes." I blurted out as we both said her father's name out loud. "This all makes so much sense! Does he know you are working with me? This is incredible!"

I had worked with a man who had always seemed to carry a layer of sadness on his heart. I could never understand the reason for his heavy heart, but at this moment, it was all unfolding before me. His daughter, the child he had given up for adoption, was sitting in my office sharing her heartbreak with me.

"How crazy is it that you know my birth father? What a small world," MacKenzie answered, shaking her head in bewilderment. She went on to explain her adoption story and all the steps she had taken to unseal the private documents. The information she had gleaned from those records were now more important than ever after death of her baby.

"Have the two of you met? I know you said you had talked to him, but have you met in person?" I asked.

"Yes, once, but we primarily communicate by email," said MacKenzie.

"I don't want to push you at all. Adoption comes with complicated feelings, and you are entitled to process all of this in your own time, but knowing both of you, I feel intuitively that there is some deep healing that needs to be done and meeting with him may be important for both of you. He is a very kind man and I know he would want to help if he could."

"I'll think about it, but first we've gotta get me pregnant," she replied. Her focus was on the future.

We ended our meeting that day with a deep sense of gratitude for coming together. The feeling I had felt from the moment I met MacKenzie now made perfect sense. Our souls were connected through old friends, and we had been put together through some divine cosmic plan to heal the physical, and energetic wounds of MacKenzie as well as those who love her.

In the fall of 2022, almost ten years to the day, MacKenzie came through my door again. I had reached out to her to discuss using her story for my book and she had excitedly agreed. When she arrived, I was thrilled to see her beautiful smile and those distinctive blue eyes again.

"You have ten years of life under your belt and the last time I saw you, you were in the middle of an incredible chapter of your story," I said.

"When we met, I was a stubborn twenty-seven-year-old who thought I had a plan, and I was going to make that plan a reality. Little did I know that life had other things in store for me," MacKenzie said.

"So much of that time is a blur for me," she continued. "I was in survival mode. Everyone thought after a blood transfusion and a couple of menstrual cycles that I was fine. I was not fine. I needed help, and I remember our Reiki session like it was yesterday. You told me I wasn't ready to get pregnant again and honestly, I was mad. I wanted that session to fix everything so I could move on."

We talked about the Reiki session and her journey through infertility, multiple pregnancies and miscarriages, and the births of her two children, which were also difficult.

"I have been through hell. I have been broken into a million pieces," she said as tears streamed down her face. "Each one of those babies broke my heart. It still aches a little more on certain days, especially on expected due dates. It's a unique grief that no one understands until you go through it."

We talked about the strength she had found in meditation and her strategies for coping with post-partum depression. Gratitude had been one of her most useful tools, meditation, and journaling had become sustaining practices.

"While I was preparing for the birth of my last child, I started using a mediation app, and one meditation resonated with me and still sustains me today. I think of a flowing river and I am a heavy rock in the river. I am not a pebble, but I am a heavy immovable rock in the river. When things feel overwhelming, I let it flow over me like water, but I remain grounded and stable. Everything flowing around me may shape me, and it may mold me, but I am that rock and I am stable."

I remembered the image of her grief as a heavy stone that I had felt within her in our Reiki session all those years ago. Perhaps the grief that had settled within her soul now holds her steady as the challenges of life move over and around her. The grounding image of the rock isn't a mystery that lurks in the background of her emotions; it appeared to her in meditation as a useful image that continues to provide peace.

"I don't take anything for granted. I hug my kids a little more on the days that I am still grieving, and I know I am incredibly lucky. They are nothing short of miracles, but honestly, when my husband got his vasectomy, I was happy. I felt safe for the first time in years. Having babies nearly killed me and I was ready to let that part of my life go."

That statement surprised me, but the point was valid. Far too many of us only want to see the bright side of a story and a happy ending. MacKenzie had two children and a good life, but the path through all of it had been harrowing.

She also shared that her infertility issues had triggered old wounds that her adoptive mom had experienced before she had adopted MacKenzie. Watching her daughter's grief and frustration reminded her of her struggles, and it brought on another entire layer of emotional trauma to the family. We never know how close to the surface those wounds are for those who love us.

"During my struggles with infertility, people kept telling me to relax and that if I stopped worrying about it, I would get pregnant. Then they told me I needed closure after I lost a baby. I didn't, and I still don't. I needed to cry and get it all out of my system, and some days I still do. I feel like my grief is like a wound with a tender little scab over it, and sometimes that scab gets bumped, and it opens again."

"I like that analogy. Humans experience grief differently and at different times, but there's no right or wrong way to process those feelings," I agreed. "It's never gone, it's just different."

I asked, "What is the state of your relationship with your birth parents? I'm still amazed that while you were going through post-partum hell, you were also processing the information in your adoption files. I can't imagine how difficult that must have been for you."

MacKenzie explained that she had met with both her birth parents separately and it was a good experience. They shared pictures and stories and got to know each other. They are not close, but they are currently in a good place.

"That's great. I had hoped it would be a source of strength and support for you," I said.

"It was and still is," she answered. "There is respect and connection, but I have very clear boundaries. My adoptive parents are my mom and dad and my children's grandparents, and my relationship with them is my priority. We are extremely close."

MacKenzie and I spent the afternoon catching up, and I felt a tremendous sense of relief that she was now in a peaceful place in her life. I look back at the first time we met ten years ago, and a million different miracles had to happen for her to walk through my door. I believe it was divinely orchestrated and when we need help, our earth angels show up. Our souls call out to those who can help us to carry our burdens through the hard times.

CHAPTER 10

ABBIE

TW: Suicide

Three weeks after I began writing this book, my dear friend died by suicide. She was thirty-eight.

I have written and rewritten this chapter and struggled to find the right words. The truth is, I am still struggling with grief. Her death has rocked me and for a while I wasn't sure if I could or should write about her. But how could I write a book about the lie of closure and not share my personal truth?

This chapter is told from my perspective, from my heart, and it is my unique journey with her. She had hundreds of friends, and many were very close to her till the end, and each will have their own stories of their life with her. She was the kind of person that left each of us with wonderful memories and the feeling of being loved.

Abbie was initially a client and then became my friend. This happens frequently, and I am always grateful that fascinating people come to me for help, and that I can build a lasting connection with them. Abbie had come to a meditation group I led at my house, and later she hired me for intuitive coaching. We used Reiki, meditation, and intuitive guidance to help her deal with issues of self-empowerment, depression, and healing of deep traumas.

The specifics of her traumas are not mine to share. I will continue to keep the details of our sessions confidential, just as I do for all my clients, living or dead. It is a commitment I gave her when our work together began, and I will not betray our contract.

I have a picture of Abbie doing yoga on the beach beside a lake. She is tall, toned, and tan, and looks like a model from a fitness magazine. She was wearing a royal blue tank top that said "Ride or Die" in big white letters. That shirt said everything you need to know about her. She was intense, loyal, and did everything full tilt.

I always felt like I needed to have a GPS tracker on her because she was always on the move. She traveled, hiked, rode her bike everywhere, and was always planning her next adventure. When a job opportunity became available to move to the mountain town that she loved so much, she took the leap. We talked about her decision to move many times and intuitively I felt it was the perfect place for her. The mountains fed her soul, and I supported her decision to relocate.

Abbie sent pictures of herself hiking on mountain trails and biking on Wyoming highways alongside herds of buffalo. She wrote blogs that told beautiful stories of her adventures. Hope and positivity filled her words. It all sounded idyllic.

When the COVID-19 lockdowns happened, Abbie had to do it alone. The small mountain town where she lived shut down, and like everyone else navigating a worldwide pandemic, she felt overwhelmed and uncertain. Then the endless months of isolation began to take a toll and worsening depression became all consuming. She knew she was in trouble, and she reached out for help.

"I haven't slept in three days," Abbie explained during a phone call. "I feel like I am outside of my body, and I don't know what to do."

"You need to call your doctor and let them know you are in crisis. This is serious. You can't continue like this," I said. We talked through a plan, and she got medication for sleep and began seeing a therapist remotely. In those months of the pandemic, everything was done remotely.

Abbie continued to struggle with depression, but she sought out opportunities to heal herself in both traditional and non-traditional methods. She embraced ecstatic dance, meditation, breath work, and yoga. She also tried psilocybin and other mind-altering substances. Each seemed to help for a short time.

On Halloween of 2021, Abbie walked up the sidewalk in front of our house amidst hundreds of ghosts and goblins. Families and children filled the neighborhood that evening, and I assumed she was with one of the children. Her appearance had changed drastically and her once radiant aura was now dimmed. I didn't see the "ride or die" girl in there anymore.

"Oh my god, I didn't even recognize you!" I admitted as we pulled up lawn chairs and welcomed her to stay and help hand out candy. She had lost weight and her face looked gaunt and pale. The change in her alarmed me, but we had only communicated by phone or text for the past few months.

"My friend, Marcie, came to Wyoming and packed me up and brought me here. I didn't trust myself to be alone anymore. I am in a dark place," she explained.

We talked about her depression, and she shared how it had become unbearable. She needed to be with other friends for her own safety. I wanted to help her, so we arranged a Reiki for a session and two days later, she returned. During our Reiki, the seriousness of her situation jarred me. As I moved my hands over her body, she felt like a hollow mannequin. Her life force was almost undetectable. Her energy was incredibly low, and I could feel her desire to leave this earth plane.

When we finished, we had a very candid conversation and I asked her if she was having suicidal thoughts.

"I'm done. I don't feel like I want to live like this anymore," she admitted. "I have tried so many different ways to feel better and nothing seems to work."

We talked for hours and agreed on some strategies to help with her feelings of hopelessness. Abbie would continue to work with her medical team and her loving team of earth angels around her. We also meditated together and called out to all our guardian angels and spirit guides to help assist her in this challenging part of her journey. I offered her a place to stay at our home, a seat at our table, and my continued support.

When she left, I felt hopeful that our session had helped, but I was also deeply concerned that she may not make it through her sadness. For several months we kept in touch, and she seemed to have highs and lows.

In April, during our last conversation, Abbie seemed like her old self. She talked about books and getting a job, and for the first time, she talked about the future. I thought she had come through the dark days and maybe she was going to pull through, but I was wrong.

On a warm June night, Abbie sent a love letter to her friends and family and gave instructions for how she wanted her death to be celebrated after she was gone, and then she died by suicide.

I was shocked when I was notified of her death. I wanted it to be different. I wanted her back and my heart was broken.

Abbie's suicide has made me question everything about myself and my own intuitive abilities. How could I not have known she would do this? Why didn't I feel her pain before it happened and reach out to her? Why hadn't I reached out to her more? Why hadn't I pushed harder when I knew she needed help? Why couldn't I stop this from happening? Should I continue doing intuitive work? Should I be writing a book to help others when I couldn't help my own friend?

It has been six months since her death, and I can't discern time. There are days it feels as though she died yesterday, and at other times, I must count the months on my fingers because I can't make sense of the dates. Grief wraps us in timelessness.

I reached out to one of Abbie's closest friends to talk about her death and decide if I should include her story in my book. Hannah had been friends with Abbie for ten years, and they were extremely close. She generously shared her journey through loving and supporting Abbie through her depression and then her own grief after Abbie died.

"I loved her so deeply. She was my person," Hannah said through tears. "I knew how deep her depression had become and I can't believe it happened."

We talked about the ironies of our relationship with Abbie and the work we do for others. Hannah lovingly works with others to create meaningful transformations through life and death, and I work with clients who are grieving and wanting to connect with their loved ones who have passed. We both felt great difficulty in returning to our work after losing our friend.

"How has being a death doula affected your own grieving process, Hannah?" I asked.

"I have been gentler with myself than I would have in the past. I see my grief as an ocean and sometimes I dip my toe into it, and on other days I am brave enough to wade in to my knees.

Sometimes it's unbearable and I cry for hours, and other days I can talk about her and feel grateful for our time together."

I explained that as a medium I had wanted to connect with her spirit right away, but it was nowhere. She was just gone. It took weeks before I heard or felt anything, and when I did it was short and very succinct. I heard the same words she had said during our last visit: "I was done." She was nowhere. Abbie was released from this earth plane, and she was no longer swimming through the deep, dark waves of depression.

In August, I felt Abbie when I stood amongst hundreds of butterfly bushes surrounding a lake in The Netherlands. Purple was her favorite color and she loved butterfly bushes. I felt her while meditating during a full moon in October, and I knew she was with me. I later felt her presence when I was performing Reiki on her friend Kate. Each of those moments felt joyful and overwhelming.

I wish I could say I have had a profound conversation with her, and she explained everything, and all my questions have been resolved, but that would be a lie. She is choosing when and where to show up for her friends, family, and me, which is the same as she did in life. She did it all on her own terms.

I want to give hope to anyone who is struggling with depression or suicidal thoughts. There is a way through your sadness, and you can allow others to support you. There are people willing to listen and love you through this. There are hundreds of options, both traditional and non-traditional, that can help you. You are not alone and there is help. The national Suicide and Crisis Lifeline is available by dialing 988.

The US National Suicide Prevention Lifeline is also available at 800-273-8255.

I want to give patience and kindness to anyone who has a friend or loved one who is living with depression. Take the time to listen, even if it feels as though you are overwhelmed by their sadness. Love is what will save you both.

I want to send love to anyone who is bereaved or impacted by suicide. Your grief is as complicated as the person who died by suicide. This grief is intense and hard. It will feel messy and overwhelming, but over time it will become less foreign to your mind and body. It will never be over or done.

Abbie,
I love you.
I miss you.
I'm sorry I couldn't do more for you.
I am here anytime you need me to listen.

CHAPTER 11

CARMEN

TW: Divorce, Infidelity

Love amongst humans is messy sometimes.

The text messages arrived at 3:30 a.m. They were from Carmen, a client I have seen in the past, which made the late-night texts mildly less annoying.

Carmen: I need to talk to you. So much is happening. I need to schedule a session with you right away.

I never answer texts in the middle of the night. Historically, middle of the night texts is always about a cheating partner, a whirlwind romance, or someone just got caught doing something very bad.

I didn't respond initially, but I remembered Carmen's emotional struggles in the past and her bouts of depression. I felt obligated to ensure her safety, so I responded.

Me: Do you feel like this is a mental health emergency?

Carmen: No. I'm just super confused. I'm dealing with some boyfriend issues.

Ding, ding, ding... We have a winner.

Carmen had consulted with me after her marriage of twelve years ended in a heartbreaking divorce. Her husband's infidelities had blindsided her, and she needed support through the first months of their separation. Carmen had been through the grief of her marriage ending and the loss of her friend network. She and her husband socialized with other couples and many of them had drifted away after the scandal of her husband's multiple affairs.

We agreed on a time in three days and in the meantime, I instructed her to just take it slow and to use the tools we had developed to move through her emotions in the past. Go outside, get some fresh air, move her body, and meditate.

Later that week, she arrived ten minutes early for her 5:30 appointment. Carmen was impeccably dressed in a navy-blue blazer and a dark green silk blouse. The color of the blouse made her gorgeous green eyes stand out. She looked like a Ralph Lauren ad.

"I've been seeing this guy and you know I have a type, and he's definitely my type. Tall, very good looking, great body, he works out a lot, and he makes me laugh," she said smiling as she spoke of him. "He is a good dad to his kids, but he just has some issues with his ex, and I don't know how to deal with it."

I began to feel a wave of hot energy flow through me and my inner sense of knowing tuned in. It's like finding a radio station on an analog radio and the signal becomes very clear. Immediately, I knew that he was not telling her the truth. I began to jot words down on a sheet of paper as our reading began:

- Red flags, thousands of them
- Painful
- Lying
- Not single. Never divorced?

I felt strongly about the man she was describing, and I watched as Carmen's energy shifted as she described him. The auric field that surrounded her shrank inward and dimmed.

"How long have they been separated?" I asked, careful to let things unfold.

"I'm not sure exactly, but over a year. He hates talking about her. He talks about how much he loves being with me because she was so controlling and she never let him do the things he enjoyed. We also have great sex, so we stay in a lot," she says with a huge smile on her face. "Our physical relationship is unlike anything I've ever experienced. I feel sexy for the first time in a long time."

"So are the two of you living together or does he just stay at your place?" I asked, knowing before she answered.

"We stay at my house. He usually must get up super early because he is a manager at a distribution center, and he must be at work by five in the morning. He also does a lot with his kids on the weekends, so he only has a limited amount of time that we can spend together," she explains. "It works out great because I'm so busy with my job that I don't need to be with him constantly. I am putting in long hours and so is he, so the limited time we do get to spend together, we really value."

"So have you ever been to his place?" I asked.

"Yes, I've been outside of it, but never inside. He says his place is a bit of a dump, and he's embarrassed of it, so he would rather come to my house." I can see a slight red flush move across her cheeks as she finishes her sentence. Her house was in an affluent neighborhood, and she had been proud of the renovations she had completed after her divorce. Her house was her sacred space.

It feels as though the giant metaphoric elephant in the room has just stepped a little closer. I can feel her energy shift again.

"Does that seem odd to you after dating for over a year?" I asked.

"Yes and no. We met during the COVID-19 stuff, and we supported each other when everyone was feeling so isolated. We chose to stay at my place because he had roommates. It has just become our routine," she explained. "I don't want to lose him. I can't go through another heartbreak," she says as her eyes fill with tears. "You know how hard my divorce was and what an emotional wreck I was for months. It took two years to get the courage up to even consider dating. I don't want to feel like that ever again."

I had witnessed her darkest days as she grieved her marriage. Her divorce had wrecked her sense of self-esteem and she had become deeply depressed, and now I could sense that this man was filling her needs in some less than healthy way.

"If you feel like he's a good guy and good person, why are you here to see me?" I asked bluntly.

She explained her feeling that things were a bit off. He accused her of blaming him for all the bad behaviors of her ex-husband, which was partially true. "We avoid discussing anything about his past, which drives me crazy. I have been an open book and I need to know the truth," she says as the tears rolled down her cheeks.

Carmen went on to share the arrangements and limitations of their relationship. She also admitted she had been helping him financially. He had told her his divorce and subsequent child support had destroyed him financially and she wanted to help him get back on his feet.

As a friend, I wanted to shake her and tell her to wake up, but as an intuitive medium, I had to allow my connection with Spirit to guide her in a way that allowed her to learn and experience the lessons her soul needed.

"If I were in a relationship with a person for a year and they had never let me come to their house, see their kids, meet their family, or see their workplace, what would you tell me?" I asked.

Carmen answered slowly, "I would tell you that it all sounds sketchy as hell and that he's definitely lying to you."

"I think you are right to trust your intuition. He might be a great guy, but if he is not willing to share all of himself with you, there's a reason. After a year together, you should know him pretty well and if you want more from the relationship, that's not a ridiculous expectation," I replied.

"So do you think he doesn't love me? Is he lying about that?" she asked as she became more quiet.

"I'm sure he loves you. Why wouldn't he? You're amazing. If I were single, I would date you. But I think there's a reason he keeps you and the rest of his life completely separate. You don't have to be psychic to see it, Carmen," I said, trying to be supportive, but brutally honest.

"What should I do?" she asked. Her voice cracked. "I don't want to push him away. I know I am still dealing with insecurities from my divorce. And I have given him a lot of money," she said through her tears.

"I know you care very deeply for him, but I feel like you need to trust your intuition. Stop giving him money. Stop letting him define all the boundaries of your relationship and insist on transparency. Treat it just like you would if you were negotiating a business deal. You are a shrewd businesswoman, and you would never be in a partnership with a business with these kinds of terms, would you?" I asked firmly. "If he is keeping absolutely everything away from you, so much so that it's keeping you awake at three o'clock in the morning, is that the kind of relationship you want to be in?"

"Am I being paranoid? Is he still in love with his ex? Are we going to get married? Is he the one?" Carmen asked as if she had reverted to an immature college freshman. Her sudden naive schoolgirl demeanor was baffling.

"Deep down, you already know the answer. You came here because you don't trust him, and no solid relationship can survive without trust. I don't think he's your guy," I said. I knew this was hard for her to hear, but I had to be truthful. If he was not willing to show her where he lives and works and where he goes when he's not with her, she would have her answer. If he was being honest, none of this would be a problem. My heart hurt for this lovely woman who wanted so badly to be loved by a good man.

"So do you think he's lying?" she asked again as if she hadn't heard anything I had just shared with her.

I could feel her energy shifting. She was putting up a wall between us. "Do *you* think he's lying?" I answered, giving her the opportunity to listen to her inner voice. Mine was tuned in loud and clear, but I wanted her to listen to her own. The right answers always come from our own sense of knowing.

She started to sob. "I think he's been lying to me all along, but I didn't want it to be true. There have been a million red flags, but I just kept looking past them and making excuses and giving him another chance. He makes me feel so good when we are together, and I don't want to be alone. I never thought I would find love again after my divorce and this gorgeous man just showed up and made me feel happy again."

"I am sure he has, but if you know there are a million red flags, you must address them. You cannot discard your sense of right and wrong. You are wise, and strong, and you deserve a partner who is your equal. Do you really feel like he's your equal? How do your friends feel about him?" I asked.

"They think he is a gorgeous asshole. None of them like him or trust him. It has taken a toll on my friendships because they say things about him that I feel are unacceptable. I am more isolated from them than I've ever been." She had created a strong circle of new friends who had become a source of stability after her divorce, and now this man was jeopardizing that too.

"Isolated, sad, worried, stressed… What are some other adjectives you would use to describe yourself as a result of your relationship with him?" I asked. "Does this sound like the kind of feelings one would have in a strong healthy relationship?"

"Why can't I find someone that I can trust? What is wrong with me?" she asked angrily.

"I'm not sure why the men you have loved haven't been honest, but you deserve to be happy. You shouldn't have to be up pacing the floor at three in the morning because you can't trust what your boyfriend is telling you. For god's sake Carmen, you are a catch, and you deserve to be treated like the goddamn goddess that you are."

She smiles through her tears and nods her head, "Why do I have to be reminded of this? You always have such a way of bringing me to the truth."

"Ted Bundy was married and had a baby with his wife while he was on death row. She knew he had been convicted of being a serial killer and she still stuck by his side. Give yourself some grace. At least you're not visiting him in prison on death row." I laughed and tried to bring some levity to the conversation. "You are going to get through this. Go find your best black bra, put it on, and start approaching this the same way you would a business negotiation. Use your power. You need transparency, facts, and an equal seat at the table. If he's not willing to negotiate fairly with you, he's got to go."

We discussed a plan for her next steps, and she left that evening more confident in her intuition. She would remain in a relationship with him only if he would be completely honest.

Six months later, Carmen returned for another reading. She arrived dressed in yoga pants and a tee shirt, her hair pulled back in a ponytail. She looked exhausted and her energy felt heavy.

"He was lying about everything," she explained. She had confronted him after our session together and he had become angry that she would trust a "crazy psychic" over him. He had agreed to some of her conditions initially, but he never followed through. Despite of his secrecy, and all the red flags, Carmen had continued with the relationship.

"I got a call from a woman who claimed to be his girlfriend. She and I have a mutual friend who had put the pieces together. Her friend told her that he was cheating and encouraged her to call me, so she did. She wanted me to know they had been living together for over a year. He had told her he worked evenings and nights, so he was gone a lot, but he was basically living with both of us. He had two women helping him financially and taking care of everything. He wasn't working at all. He is a fucking piece of shit," she said angrily.

I didn't disagree with her description of him. Those behaviors were deplorable. All the negative energy I had felt about him in our last session had been accurate.

"How could I have been so gullible? Why did I trust him?" Carmen's questions no longer came from a place of sadness. They were now laced with venom.

We talked about the confrontation and the ugliness of his lies. She had been hurt deeply—again. We discussed the need to nurture and trust her intuition, even if the guy is incredibly tall, and handsome, and the sex is great. Our need to be wanted and connected can make us blind to the flaws of others. She agreed to take some time for herself to grieve the end of this relationship.

"When those red flags are waving in front of your face, it's for a reason," I said. "Love makes us feel crazy sometimes." Our inner sense of knowing doesn't mislead us when it comes to protecting our highest self. Our angels and our guides really are giving us every opportunity to listen to that guidance. Carmen knew he wasn't trustworthy from very early on in their relationship, but she wanted him to fix a broken part of herself.

We talked about her pain and created a plan for her to begin the work of healing again. I hugged her before she walked out the door.

"Thank you. I'm feeling a million things right now, but I feel better. At least I know I was right to not trust him, and I should have listened to my inner voice. I'll never do that again," she said.

We all make mistakes. We can get swept up in the energy of another and lose sight of our values and boundaries. Sometimes we enter relationships because we are desperate to fulfill our needs to be partnered or to create a family, and it's not the right person for us. And sometimes we pick people that show us they aren't trustworthy; we see a million red flags and we just bulldoze our way past them in hopes that this person will be "the one." Those two words drive people to some really insane places. It is painful and grieving a broken heart takes time.

The grief of a divorce or break up is no different than the grief after a death. It is deep and painful. If not processed, the pain of separation can throw us into unhealthy relationships that fill our need to be wanted and worthy of love again. It can become a vicious cycle if we don't use what our partners teach us and grow from those lessons.

Every relationship isn't meant to last forever, but somehow that has become the expectation. Romantic love is fleeting, but the love that comes with trust, respect, and honesty can persevere. Sometimes relationships can be a past-life connection or pattern that our soul needs to resolve. It all makes life as a human complicated, emotional, and messy.

Part of my work as an intuitive guide is to bring attention to the massive elephants in the room and be truthful about said elephants. It's not easy, because humans want to hear the truth only if it matches the romantic storyline they have created. Sometimes that storyline is great, but real life is never a fairytale.

CHAPTER 12

PAUL

TW: Death of a Sibling

Every once in a while, something magical happens. On a bus or a plane, we meet a random stranger, introduce ourselves to our seatmate, and within no time we have shared our most intimate hopes and dreams. A captive audience for a short time, willing to listen to the unedited version of our story. Perhaps we are all just waiting for the right opportunity to be heard.

Talking with Paul felt like a conversation with an old friend. His soothing, low voice conveyed an energy of comfortable confidence and sage wisdom that comes from decades of working with patients as a therapist and a shaman. I had been connected with Paul through a mutual friend and planned to interview him for my book. It was supposed to be a brief Zoom interview, but we ended up talking for over an hour. My intention for our conversation was to tap into his varied scope of expertise and years of experience in the fields of creativity, innovation, and therapy. Little did I know he would share with me one of the most intimate and poignant moments of his life.

As our conversation began, I said, "I'm exploring the concept of closure, which in my opinion is a word that is manipulative and overused."

"What do you mean? Closure as in closing a deal?" Paul asked.

"No, as an ending to uncomfortable feelings. After something difficult happens, like a death, a crime, or a loss, people will say they need an answer to a specific question. There is a belief that to accept a death, we need an open casket and a funeral so we can get closure, or something very definitive, but I believe that closure is a non-existent state of being. It's just not true. Is there a story or something that comes to mind for you when I say that?"

Paul leaned forward and placed his elbows on the desk. He looked as though he had just come inside from a hike, his salt-and-pepper hair slightly tousled. He was dressed casually, still in a plaid flannel, which was unbuttoned and hung loosely open to show a simple tee shirt underneath. Raw wood planks surround him on the angled ceiling and walls of the room in the A-frame house he had built himself. He looked as though he was sitting inside of one of the trees in the forests that surround his home in upstate New York.

"I think closure is the wrong metaphor in a way because what are you closing? What are you doing? You're integrating something into your psyche, and it then becomes a story you can comfortably tell," Paul answered.

As I listened, I felt an immediate energetic shift, like a deep pulling from my throat down into my chest and sensation of shortness of breath. I wasn't trying to do a reading with Paul, but I felt something very traumatic had happened in his past.

"My brother died in a terrible car crash. I saw his body when he was dead, but the real truth is it took me a couple of years to integrate his death into my being. I'm still surprised at grief showing up here and there," he said calmly. "If we sought integration as elders, or as those that have gone through a type of closure, we could tell people that this will take time. You'll integrate it into your psyche, and the goal really is to get to the place where you can comfortably tell the story and it doesn't carry a huge emotional load. You can talk about it without making everybody around you uncomfortable."

I was a little taken aback by his thoughts about the need to make sure others feel comfortable, but grief and sadness cause many to feel vulnerable. I believe most of us carry some aspects of grief within us, and I had never thought about the possibility that part of the healing process meant only sharing our grief in a way that is socially acceptable. Do we filter our true feelings to maintain the ease of a conversation, even though it may not benefit us? Do we stop sharing our grief because societal rules dictate that we must not make someone else sad?

He continued, "Grief is integrated when you can use your story to help someone else whose grief is still fresh for them, or you choose to not say anything, because you know they have to go through their own process."

This, I thought, was the conundrum of the human experience. We always feel the need to say something because we are unable to handle the long, uncomfortable pauses in conversations that involve grief. Silence is socially awkward and sometimes perceived as cold or uncaring. I told him about the research I had done about cultural rituals around death and how that might change the experience for the bereaved.

For instance, in America, after someone dies, the family and friends have nothing to do with preparing the body for burial; instead, we are burdened with either going to the cemetery or figuring out what to do with ashes. In other cultures, there are rituals or activities after death that involve family members. They take part in bathing and caring for the body and there are specific time frames for burial and grieving. By contrast, in the United States, we have just gotten further away from the process, so it adds to the emotional disconnect

Paul paused for a moment. "That's interesting," he said. "The purpose of all of these rites of passages is to move from one state of being to another and to integrate this new perspective into your psyche."

He explained that these rites of passage—not only those related to death, but to life, marriage, and other experiences that make up adulthood—are so powerful because they involve some level of challenge. Integrating these experiences as a new way of being necessitates growth that can only come from pain. I had been scribbling down all these pearls of wisdom as Paul was talking, but with this next sentence, I put my pen down, stopped taking notes, and gave him my full attention.

"My brother, Scott, was in the Navy, had PTSD, and alcoholism, and he crashed his car into a lake by accident. He had head trauma and drowned. After my brother's death, my wife and I flew to Virginia to be with my parents. As the four of us sat around the kitchen table, I realized that Dad was just kind of holding all this in. He is from the generation of men who lived through the Second World War, who don't show emotions. I knew that it would be helpful for him if I could show my own grief. I knew if he could integrate it, he wouldn't have to repress it or push it aside." His voice softened.

"I was casting about in my mind as a therapist and rite-of-passage shaman guide and I was trying to think of what to do so that Dad could integrate this, and it just came to me. We needed to go dig the grave ourselves," he said enthusiastically.

What? My mind was trying to make sense of what I just heard. Typically, when we hear of someone picking up a shovel and digging a grave, it's usually part of a Dateline episode. I was riveted to my computer screen. I couldn't possibly imagine where this story was going.

"We grew up Catholic, and my mom and dad were still very active in the Catholic church, and I thought maybe we'd be able to pull some strings so we could go in and hand dig this grave. All of this went through my mind in a heartbeat, and I looked at my dad and I said, 'we're gonna dig Scott's grave.'"

He continued, "We had to do a lot of paperwork and we had to call in some favors, but we got permission. It was as challenging as you can imagine, and then we dug that fricking grave."

"I didn't know that was possible. I guess it's something I would never have considered," I said. "I assumed there were laws surrounding burials, but honestly it's never come up in a conversation before."

"My brother's plot was close to a tree, which seems idyllic before you have to dig down through all of the roots. The soil was clay in that area, which made it even harder."

As he spoke, his tone changed from the softness he had felt for his father to the frustration he felt for his dead brother.

"My father, my surviving brother, and I, we're all together, digging and digging, and it was absolutely miserable." He paused for a moment. "I don't tell this to many people."

Hearing him say that surprised me, and I felt incredibly honored that he was willing to share it with me. One of my gifts as an intuitive is to be fully present and listen. I hear hundreds of stories each year from my clients, and I never take the trust that has been given to me for granted. Sessions are not always about trying to connect with a loved one who has passed or to see something from another realm. It's about being still and open and allowing another human to unburden their heart.

"We laughed, and we cried, and we just kept digging. When we finally got to the bottom of that grave we had been digging for hours, we were covered in sweat and mud and by that point, we were mad. Our anger was what drove us to finish at that point. My dad is older, so he was up above and watched us finish. My brother, Jack, and I were down in this deep hole, and I turned to Jack, and I started yelling, 'Piss on you, Scott!' You aren't supposed to be angry at the person who died, but our rage needs to be released. We started yelling all kinds of profanities and we really let Scott have it. That grave was where we needed to leave our pain."

Paul went on, "About six months later, I was staying in a hotel and there was a movie on TV about Navy Seals, and it triggered my grief, and I started sobbing. The movie ended and I was still sobbing, and it must have been very loud, because there was a knock on my door. This kind woman had heard me crying and came and offered help if I needed it. I assured her I was okay, just going through some emotions in that moment. I must have sounded bad from the other side of the wall, but I've done this work enough with myself and others that you do what you need to do to integrate it into your psyche or to grieve it, but at that point, I think I was not fully integrated."

"So, despite the monumental rite of passage you completed with your father and brother, your grief still needed to be expressed. Those hard moments come, whether we think we are finished with our grief or not," I replied.

"I haven't shared this story. Talking about digging the grave brought tears to my eyes just now, but they weren't for my brother who died. It was more about the bonding I shared with my dad and my surviving brother."

I was still trying to process what he has just shared with me. People share many of their deep, dark traumas in our intuitive sessions, but this story was very unique. I felt his pain from a deep heart space, and I am amazed by his family's journey through grief.

I tried to gather my thoughts after Paul's deeply moving story and redirect the conversation to Paul's expertise in shamanism. "Okay, imagine three chairs. One is your therapist chair, another is your shaman's chair, and the other is the think tank and innovations chair. Sit in the shamanic chair and tell me what closure means to you."

Paul thought for a moment, "In shamanic language, you receive wisdom from the upper world and the lower world, and you bring it into your psyche. You've listened to what non-ordinary reality has to teach you and the elders—the other living things, the rocks, the plants, the trees—they're all from a shamanic point of view. They're all alive and you've been able to listen to whatever it is they have to tell you and that's not ordinary reality. It's a much different journey versus a traditional ceremony where the funeral director says a prayer, or a Catholic priest sprinkles the holy water on the casket. Ordinary reality and ritual is useful, depending on your background and what works for you. Like hanging the cloth over the mirrors or turning the pictures or the mirrors around, as we see in the Jewish tradition, it's all ordinary reality."

Paul explained that in shamanic journeys, the shaman opening a ceremony takes the journey for you. The shaman uses drumming techniques for entering into another world by breathing or chanting. You accompany the shaman and state the intention for the journey. Perhaps there is a specific issue you are trying to resolve, or an issue that is causing you emotional pain. The shaman enters the mystic world and asks the question for you, and through that journey, you obtain an answer.

"Often in the upper world, the message comes as language. In the lower world, it's more often from nature. As we journey, I would explain what I see and what I am experiencing and give you the wisdom I have received. When the journey is complete, you would have an integration."

It was easy to visualize myself on a shamanic journey with Paul as my guide. He has taken hundreds of individuals on sacred journeys throughout his career, and I quickly see the wisdom emerging from the story he has shared about his brother's death. To integrate their grief, Paul took his family on a physical shamanic journey into the earth, taking upon themselves the heroic act of digging a grave. With the first shovel of dirt, they discovered the soil was thick, sticky, and laden with tree roots. The soil and trees gave them sacred wisdom. From the surface, a headstone near a shade tree sounds idyllic, but the reality of fighting with the roots is as hard to cut through as the complex tangles of family trauma. What emerged from their journey into the underworld was laughter, sadness, tears, pain, and rage.

Grief and loss are complex and absolutely miserable at times. The emotions that cycle through us don't wait till the perfect moment to begin or end, and anything can trigger a memory that pulls us right back into our grief. Despite Paul being a wise man, shaman, and therapist, grief found him in a hotel room and a movie triggered his pain again.

Grief shows up when we least expect it. Sometimes we can handle it and other times it buries us, but we must allow it. There is no way around it and no ending for love that has nowhere to go. We must let it out so that over time, we can integrate it and feel more comfortable with it.

We also must let go of the need to filter our feelings of grief in conversation. It may be socially awkward, but we must begin to honor all feelings and allow others to see our truth.

CHAPTER 13

ALEX AND KATE

TW: Death of a Parent

Sometimes it can take years for things or events that I see in intuitive readings to make sense. Sometimes I am wrong, but most of the time I'm right.

"Are you planning to sell your shop?" It was the first thing that popped into my mind as I sat down for a reading with my new client.

"No, absolutely not," Alex replied with certainty.

"Are you sure? You're not thinking of moving or relocating? That's the first thing I'm getting," I replied.

I had never met Alex before, and it was our first intuitive session together. She sat in my sunroom with the summer light shining off her curly hair. Her beautiful blue eyes searching for some reason that I would ask such a silly question.

"I have a super successful business that I love, a daughter in grade school, and I love my house. I am absolutely positive that I am not moving."

"Okay, that's weird. It feels really clear to me, but I could be off. Let's move on," I answered, allowing myself to reset so I could continue. By the end of our hour together we had connected with her grandmother, and a friend from high school who had died in a car accident, and laughed about some stories from her youth.

I continued to work with Alex for two years as a client for Reiki and intuitive sessions and grew to love my time with her. She was a firecracker in every sense of the word.

One fall morning, I got a text from her that read, "I need to see you as soon as possible." I get those types of messages from clients frequently, but never from Alex. I felt a hot flush go through my body as I thought of her. I immediately knew something serious was happening and she needed help.

We arranged for a time to meet for a reading and when Alex walked through my door, I immediately felt her fear and sadness. It moved inside me like a wave of nausea. I welcomed her into the living room, and she took a seat on the couch. Immediately, my dog, Dixie, jumped up to join her. Dixie, a terrier mix, is also quite sensitive and joins in as an emotional support dog during sessions. Thousands of tears have fallen onto her scruffy fur over the years.

"I am freaking out," Alex blurted out immediately. "I am so stressed, and I don't know what to do."

"Let's start at the beginning," I said calmly. I began to use my energy to guide her toward grounding and calm the situation, but Alex's heart and mind were racing, and I could feel that something devastating had happened

"It's my mom. She has been feeling sick and having trouble with her stomach for the past couple of months. She went to her local doctor, and she was told that it was reflux and nothing to worry about. It never improved with medication, so while they were here visiting, her pain got much worse. I made her go to the E.R. at UNMC and within thirty minutes they had diagnosed her with pancreatic cancer." Alex's face was flushed, and the tears were pouring from her eyes. "How the fuck did her doctor not find this sooner?"

"Oh, Alex, that is awful. I am so sorry." I knew the outcomes for pancreatic cancer are not good and I felt a deep sense of dread as Alex spoke about her mother. I hoped I was wrong, or too close to the situation and feeling Alex's sorrow myself. I had met her mom, Kate, and she was a lovely woman. She and I were both the same age, so the possibility of her dying was hard to imagine.

"What am I going to do without her? How am I supposed to live without my mom?" Alex stroked Dixie's head as she wept.

"Let's stay focused on today and what you can do now for her and for yourself. Therapies and treatments are getting better every day and she is tough enough to survive this. I am here to support you so you can support her."

"I am so angry. I am so mad that this is happening to my mom, and I can't do anything," she cried. "She doesn't deserve this. She is the kindest person I know; she takes care of everyone. I don't want to lose her. I can't lose her!"

"You have every right to be mad, and let's stay mad. It will help get things moving. Most importantly, let's stay calm when you are with your mom. I can help you do that. Alex, I know this feels impossible, but you can do this," I said, knowing Alex would need support as she went through this devastating experience.

"I can't live without her. She drives me crazy, and I don't answer her texts half of the time, and I know I should. I never imagined this could happen," Alex sobbed as she spoke. "What do you see? Is my mom going to die?"

"I don't know. I can't say for sure, but let's focus on what we do know and deal with what's at hand," I answered in complete honesty. I didn't know for sure that Kate would live or die, but I knew that Alex needed all the love and support I could give her.

Three months later, Kate died peacefully with her family by her side.

Alex and I had developed a friendship and I sent her energy with distance Reiki as she grieved her mother's death. When we were together, we talked about her sadness and grief. She felt lost at times and questioned everything, but she had to continue living because she had a child, a business, and a life to live.

One evening, I checked in on Alex because I felt intuitively that she was having a hard day.

"When am I going to stop feeling this way? I feel completely broken," she asked with frustration.

"Never. You will never not grieve for your mom. That love never ends and the two of you are both so deeply connected. It will get easier with time, but it's never over," I said, knowing the truth was better than some silly cliche about time passing and wounds healing,

"Do you see her? Does she have anything she wants to tell me?" Alex asked.

At that moment, a very clear answer popped into my head, the toilet. "This is going to sound weird, but I am seeing a toilet. Do you feel like you talk to her when you're sitting on the toilet?"

"No, not at all. I never hear messages from her. I have seen her in a dream, but I would give anything to hear her voice."

"I am clearly seeing a toilet, and she is showing me that she is there with you in the bathroom," I said.

"Oh my god!" Alex exclaimed. "I have a picture of my mom pushing my brother in a stroller at Disneyland and it's hanging over my toilet. She has a can of Coke in one hand and a cigarette in the other. It captured her perfectly! She hated that picture, and she always wanted me to take it down."

"She definitely still has an opinion about that picture. She is with you even if you don't feel her," I said. "I feel like she was so stubborn in life that she isn't going to pop in as some sparkly angel. She is going to do it her way. A cigarette and a snarky look on her face is definitely how she is coming through."

"She constantly nagged at me about keeping my bathroom clean. I hated it when she asked me how long it had been since I cleaned my shower. We argued over my cleaning all the time. I don't know what stage of grief this is, but I miss her so much. I would love to hear her yell at me about my shower one more time."

"There aren't stages, and your grief is happening as it is supposed to. The alleged stages don't really describe how we are to grieve, and it can change from minute to minute. Just like you and your mom did with each other while she was here on this earth plane," I said, still smiling about the funny way our loved ones show up to bring us confirmation and loving support.

Kate had died quickly after her diagnosis and far too soon. Her rapid decline and death had been devastating for her friends and family to experience. She had been snatched away by cancer. No one had time to process or feel, until the silent weeks after she was gone. The immense pain Alex had shared with me could never be resolved by the illusion of closure. Her mother was bigger than life, and her spirit is still, unlimited, and radiant.

Two years after her mother's death, Alex came to me again for an intuitive reading, but this time it was to discuss her life path. She was not sure about the next steps, but her heart was no longer in running her business, her father had relocated, and she was considering moving to be closer to him.

"Do you think this is the time for me to go?" she asked.

"Do you remember the first question I asked you when we met?"

"No, I don't."

"I asked if you were closing your business and moving," I shared smiling. "You were pretty salty about it, but it was coming through so clear that I asked you twice."

"Are you kidding me? I don't remember that. So you saw this all those years ago? Wow! I never thought I would want to leave, but I just can't do this anymore. I'm so tired and ready for a change," Alex answered.

"It's time. It's okay for you to move forward and for you to stay close to your father. He needs you and you need him. It's going to be okay," I told her, feeling certain that the messages I shared were for the greatest good of Alex and her family. It had taken five years for that first moment of our time together to make sense and now it was finally a reality. "You are all still grieving your mom, but she will be there with you every step of the way and in every room of your new house. Even the bathroom."

Sometimes in readings, messages come through clearly and make sense, and sometimes they don't. My job is to share them and trust that all will be revealed in time because I am only a conduit. I feel privileged to walk beside clients and friends as they navigate the challenges in life and even more grateful when I can help unburden a grieving heart. It's different for everyone and I am here to hold space for that unending love that binds us together.

PART III

TOOLS, TECHNIQUES, AND FRIENDLY ADVICE FOR DEALING WITH GRIEF

In Part 3, I share tools and helpful advice for dealing with the spectrum of emotions we experience as we grieve. These tools can be used simultaneously or individually, but all are meant to bring comfort and healing,

CHAPTER 14

TOOLS, TECHNIQUES, AND FRIENDLY ADVICE FOR DEALING WITH GRIEF

Through years of self-discovery and client work, I have gathered tools and techniques that can be helpful in dealing with grief. These suggestions are not in any order for use, and they can be implemented independently or shared with others. There is no simple easy answer to the pain of loss, but these tools and words of wisdom can help you through it.

1. **Meditation:** Meditation works and anyone can do it. It is simply taking a moment and becoming still. It allows us time to be with whatever it is that we are feeling. If you are new to meditation, start with a guided version. It's like having someone guide us into a room and welcome us to the new place in our mind versus trying to start something new by running into our new practice while dragging a bag

of wild cats and no idea how to calm them. It takes time and practice, but it is a discipline that has been studied, replicated, and proven to have massive benefits.

2. **Breathwork:** Find a comfortable quiet place to sit or lie down for five minutes every day. Take slow deep breaths and focus only on your breathing. This simple act allows our nervous system to relax and our body to move out of fight or flight mode. If your mind wanders, use a phrase to reset your thoughts, but keep it simple. I use phrases or a mantra that are short, like "I am" or "I am love."

3. **Give Your Grief a Name:** There is no easy way around grief. It is constantly changing and forever yours. It will be different, but it's never gone. Allowing ourselves to know grief and all of its dimensions is no different than knowing happiness. We have a million words for utter joy, but few for grief. Seek the words that name your feelings and use them in conversation. The more frequently we share our feelings honestly, the easier it becomes.

4. **Acknowledge the Grief in Others:** If you can see the pain in someone's eyes or feel it on their soul, say something. Let's all stop avoiding every part of our fellow man. The good, the bad, and the difficult are worthy of our time and attention. Just one kind word can change the trajectory of someone's life. We are all seeking connection and validation even in its simplest form.

5. **Therapy:** Therapy and counseling do work. There are many different techniques available to support us as we move through the challenges of life. If you don't feel

supported and connected to your therapist in a way that matches your needs, find a new one. There are hundreds of options out there and you can find the right match. Hypnotherapy, EMDR, expressive art therapy, and sound healing are all non-traditional and effective modalities. Be open to new options.

6. **Some Mediums Are Good:** Mediums and psychics can be helpful in finding some of the answers you may be seeking, but they cannot give you closure. They can provide insights and information which may give you some sense of clarity and direction. If you have been going to see them over and over, and you still aren't feeling any better, it's time to stop. Try something different. When you find a good one, you will know.

7. **Suicide Hotline:** If you are feeling that you no longer want to live or are having thoughts of suicide, reach out now. There is support and there are hotlines available twenty-four hours a day. The United States has a twenty-four-hour suicide crisis hotline that can be accessed by dialing **988** on your phone. The US National Suicide Prevention Lifeline is also available at 800-273-8255. Tell someone, anyone, what you are feeling and let yourself get help.

8. **The Stages of Grief:** There are no specific stages of death and dying, grief or grieving. There are no rules when it comes to our emotional responses to grief. There is no right or wrong way, no timeline to grieve, and that's okay. We don't need a framework for being human. We need grace, love, and support. And sometimes cake. Cake makes a lot of things feel better.

9. **Get Those Words Out of Your Head:** Words have power and letting them swirl in our head can become overwhelming. Give your thoughts and feelings a place to land. Your truth may feel vulnerable, but it needs to be released. Write it in a letter, keep a journal, create a blog, or talk to someone. Getting our emotions out on paper or as a spoken word frees up space within our mind. It doesn't have to be epic or perfect; it just needs to be released.

10. **Try Something Different:** Something may work one day but not the next. Just as the seasons change, so do our preferences. Sometimes I use music with my meditations, and other times it drives me crazy. Be open to adjusting your tools and techniques. Look for new teachers or classes that interest you and give yourself the opportunity to try new healing techniques. There are hundreds of ways to expand your repertoire.

11. **Social Media Avoidance:** Social media can be a black hole for self-judgment and it can feed insecurities and unrealistic expectations. Remember social media is curated and targeted to keep us feeling insecure or sad. Do not let it be a way to numb yourself or disappear. We are all seeking connection and community, and if it is not genuinely creating that for you, get off of it! Use a timer or an app to limit your time on your phone. Stepping away from our devices allows us to connect with the rest of the world, and in the world, magical things happen.

12. **Grounding Techniques:** The earth is under our feet and always with us, but rarely do we actually touch it. We are in shoes, on sidewalks, in buildings or cars, and the skin

of our body rarely connects with the ground. There is a magnetic frequency of the earth that is naturally calming, and it can help to settle us when we are feeling anxious, stressed, or out of balance. It is free and it is always available, so go outside, take off your shoes, and sit in the grass. Walk barefoot on a dirt path. Lie down on the ground and let yourself connect with the earth.

13. **Aromatherapy:** Smell is a powerful sense and aromatherapy can be a simple way to shift feelings and emotions. Just as a specific smell can trigger the memory of a loved one, an essential oil, incense, or aroma can move us to a different emotional state. Play with scents or consult an aromatherapist for a specific oil blend that matches your needs.

14. **Messages:** Prayer, meditation, or connection with God, Goddess, the Universe, or the Collective Consciousness are beautiful ways to receive messages reminding us that we are not alone. There are millions of souls, angels, spirit guides, and energies around us at all times and these helping spirits are pure love. They are never far from us, so ask them directly for help and guidance. Our loved ones who have passed want to be part of our lives and when we allow ourselves to have a connection and conversation with them, it soothes our heart and our mind.

15. **Move Your Body:** Do something physically challenging to release your grief. Hike a mountain, build something, run, walk a marathon, go skydiving, learn to belly dance, or go whitewater rafting. Monumental acts, heroic acts, and physical challenges give us new markers within our

neural pathways and help us reframe the timeline of our life. We can dedicate these challenges to our loved ones, or we can simply do it for ourselves, but doing something out of the ordinary can help us find our way back to the new version of ourselves. We can never be the same after loss, but we can be a different and wonderful version of ourselves.

16. **Cultivate Creativity and Inspiration**: Art, music, dance, anything that moves you to feel a sense of energy that inspires you. We can grieve and grow simultaneously. It is okay to express your feelings of joy and happiness and feel alive.

17. **Explore Your Own Intuitive Abilities:** If you feel that you are intuitive or have psychic abilities, you do. We are all born with gifts and over time we learn to distrust those abilities. You don't have to make a declaration to the world that you are intuitive, just begin to see the magic that is unfolding around you. Sometimes the loss of someone or an experience of grief can bring those abilities to the forefront, and it can feel scary or overwhelming. Take your time, meditate, and allow it to unfold in a way that feels right for you. If you need help or want a mentor, send it up to your angels and let them bring the right person to you. It can happen for you as it did for me.

It is my hope that one or more of these tools or suggestions will help you in some way. They can be used simultaneously or individually, but my intention is that they support you as if I were standing beside you holding your hand through your pain.

CONCLUSION

There is something good that comes with aging. Rarely in our youth-obsessed culture is it celebrated, but the passage of time allows us to collect experiences. We get to taste, feel, dance, cry, laugh, rage, know great love and the pain of heartbreak. We get to swim in the vast ocean of human emotions. We get to see the good and bad of our fellow human beings, and if we are still and willing to rise above our ego for just a moment, we can see the beauty in all of it.

When I first began writing this book several years ago, I was sure of the message that I needed to share. I felt compelled to tell the stories of my life and of the sessions with my clients, and to lift others up with my words, but something held me back. I blamed it on insecurities, procrastination, and self-sabotage. I scribbled and typed, but nothing came together, but now I know I was still gathering information and learning hard lessons about grief myself.

A lived experience is different. It requires immersion, swallowing, digestion, intimacy, and communion. Mother Nature gave me that experience and it changed my view of everything. Her fury washed away my certainty. Water shook my sense of direction, and it diluted my sense of trust. I thought I had compassion for the struggles that come with PTSD and that I understood the power of memory and reality blurring at the mention of a name, or a weather report. It's different now that it is my own.

I thought I knew fear and compassion intimately until the pandemic of 2020 and the death of millions sent massive waves of grief across the universe. It changed the way I saw my fellow humans. The audacity of people I once called friends to deny the deaths of others due to COVID-19 was shocking. The mob mentality and politicization of the pandemic made me doubt humanity and broke my heart. The initial isolation was imposed, then embraced, and then it became hard to reintegrate into society. The distrust that had rooted itself so deeply in my soul after the flood became more powerful with COVID-19 and I know was not alone. Now, two years later, the division amongst my fellow citizens is still as deep as the Grand Canyon.

I know the murky colors that emerged in the auric field of someone that had no desire to live any longer. The summer of 2022, my friend died by suicide. I thought I could help her in a way that would keep her here on this earth plane, but I couldn't. I thought I could use all the tools that I know to help her see a future, to buoy her up and be a lighthouse for her. I thought I could give her the strength to swim to shore when she felt like she was drowning in her emotions, but I couldn't. She was tired, she made her decision, and now she is free. I miss her terribly.

Through the many conversations I have had with those who have participated in the writing of this book, one common thread has emerged: When we are sad, we don't want to make others uncomfortable with our sadness. We don't want others to have to bear the weight of our heartache, so we stop talking about it. We swallow our pain and suffer in silence. We don't want to burden our friends and family.

Our societal norms don't embrace grieving that is too long, too loud, or too complicated. We like things neat, tidy, quick, and clean. We are to emulate Jackie Kennedy in her pink dress and pill box hat, standing defiant and stoic. Our societal norms allow short, specific rituals for grieving, and after the allotted days, we slather on the cliches. Get over it, turn that frown upside down, time to move on. We don't have patience with sadness and depression. We must do better.

Grief, sadness, and emotions are as complicated as the galaxy that we inhabit. There are no hard rules or structures in the mysteries of the universe and the same applies to the human experience. There is no such thing as closure. It is a lie. It is a mythical term that has given us a false hope of an ending to our pain. It has been overused and this book is your permission slip to let it go.

I hope that through these stories you have found something that has brought you comfort and honored your soul. I hope that if you are feeling overwhelmed or stuck in your grief, this book can lift you just a little. I hope that this book reminds you that you are not alone, your grief is beautiful, and being a human is messy.

ACKNOWLEDGMENTS

Writing a book is never a solitary effort and this holds true for *Closure: The Lie We Tell Ourselves*. It is with great pleasure that I acknowledge the support, encouragement and contributions of the many individuals who helped make this project a reality.

First and foremost, I would like to express my profound gratitude to my husband Ryan, whose support has been unwavering. Thank you for being open and willing to walk beside me as I scaled my "Everest." This project has been years in the making and I could not have felt my way through these deeply emotional chapters without your love. Thank you for keeping the home fires burning and never letting me throw in the towel. I couldn't have done it without you.

Thank you to my family and friends, who have been my constant source of inspiration and motivation throughout this journey. Their unwavering support and belief in me have been invaluable. I am deeply grateful for their love and encouragement. Molly, Colton, Kyle, Jacy, Waylon, Carter, and Frannie Jo, your love for me has been the light that guided me through the dark moments.

I would also like to thank my editor and publisher, New Degree Press, who provided me with the guidance and support I needed to transform my manuscript into a finished book. To my editors, Katie Siegler and Chrissy Wolfe, thank you for helping me turn a bunch of sad stories into a book that I am incredibly proud of.

Thank you to Pam Young, Barb Hannon, Teri Culbertson, Pat Ahrendsen, and Leia Baez. Thank you for wading through the revisions with me. Your feedback was invaluable, and these chapters are better because of your wisdom.

A huge debt of gratitude to my sweet friend Mary Baak. Your brilliant edits and insights have been the magic dust that needed to be sprinkled amongst these pages.

Finally, I am grateful to the many clients, friends and students who have allowed me to share your stories. Without your willingness to share your grief this book would not exist. Your feedback and support have been a source of inspiration, and I hope that this book will be a valuable tool for understanding grief and the need to let go of the myth of closure.

A special thank you to everyone who pre-ordered a copy of my book and donated to my pre-launch campaign. Thank you very much for reminding me there are so many people in my community who love and care about me. I donated a portion of the proceeds of the pre-sale campaign to

MS Forward, allowing the loving intentions of this book to be shared on an even grander scale.

Anna Nance
Lisa Jenkins
Mary Baak
Imogen Dalton Hope
Nancy Movall
Dee Luttrell
Leia Baez
Pat Ahrendsen
Darci Isherwood
Cindy Bussey
Barbara Hannon
Mary Knabe
Judith Sexton
Katrina Wells
Janelle Baber
Patti Hasty
Carol Cox
Ryan Isherwood
Natalie Riggs
Emilee Eggert
Julie Zoucha
Teri Culbertson
Molly O'Neil
Ann McAndrews
Tina Kaeding
Amy Peterson
Kimberly Treacy
Carly Cummings
Adam Gomez

Meg Kennelly
Sarah Riggs
Darlene Austin
Juli Coppersmith
Amy Renken
Kathleen Turco
Barb LeMoine
Sheralyn Jarvis
Tanja Shelton
Lisa McNeel
Karen Lepp
Leressa Joiner
Jennifer Butterbaugh
Berk Brown
Rebecca Olander
Betti Thomasian
Angella Arndt
Tabitha Cooper
Cristina Toth
Victor Murray
Mayra Murguia
Kelley Patton
Valerie Delk
Dave Palcic
Chaeli Souvannasoth
Susie Keith
Jodi Stice
Ana Armstrong
Kimberlee Faughn

Beth Powers
Susan Yager
Timothy Reeder
Lori Lemmers
Traci Janousek
Caryn Grazier

Chris Kopp
Pamela Young
Kari Dauner
Teresa Hawk
Khrystyna Heberer
Kim Jarecki

APPENDIX

INTRODUCTION

Bevan, Richard. n.d. "The Magical Life of Dr. Dee, Queen Elizabeth I's Royal Astrologer." History.com. Accessed February 22, 2023.
https://www.history.com.uk/articles/the-magical-life-of-dr-dee-queen-elizabeth-i-s-royal-astrologer.

Groeneveld, Emma. 2018. "Runes Definition." World History Encyclopedia. June 19, 2018. Accessed February 22, 2023.
https://www.worldhistory.org/runes.

IBISWorld. 2021. "Psychic Services in the US: Market Size 2005-2027." IBISWorld. Updated: April 9, 2021. Accessed February 22, 2023.
https://www.ibisworld.com/industry-statistics/market-size/psychic-services-united-states/.

CHAPTER 3

Cambridge Dictionary. s.v. "Closure." Accessed February 22, 2023.
https://dictionary.cambridge.org/dictionary/english/closure.

Cherry, K. 2021. "Gestalt Laws of Perceptual Organization" Verywell Mind. Updated April 25, 2021. Accessed February 26, 2023. https://www.verywellmind.com/gestalt-laws-of-perceptual-organization-279835.

Kubler-Ross, Elisabeth. 1969. *On Death and Dying.* New York: Simon and Schuster.

Madeira, Jody. 2012. *Killing McVeigh,* New York: New York University Press.

National Funeral Directors Association. n.d. "Statistics." NFDA. Accessed February 22, 2023. https://ndfa.org/news/statistics.

CHAPTER 7

Stiene, Bronwen, and Frans Stiene. 2005. *The Japanese Art of Reiki: A Practical Guide to Self Healing.* Hants, UK: Hunt.